Domestic Violence and Children

What can schools and social care workers do to help children affected by domestic violence?

Large numbers of children are affected by domestic violence. The problem crosses every social class and culture. It causes distress and anxiety in children and adversely affects their learning and play, as well as their behaviour, well-being and school attendance.

Education professionals may know of a child or family in crisis and want to help, yet feel outside their comfort zone, grappling with a complex issue not covered in their training. This book describes the impact of domestic violence on children and provides support for education and social care professionals. It takes heavy workloads into account and suggests practical ways of meeting the needs of pupils who come from difficult home backgrounds.

The authors provide guidance and advice on:

* identifying and responding to signs of distress
* helping pupils to talk about and make sense of their experiences
* the impact of domestic violence on parenting and how parents can be supported
* the needs of young people in refuges and temporary accommodation
* pupil safety and government safeguarding guidelines
* educating young people and the community about domestic violence
* specialist domestic violence services and other agencies that support schools.

Domestic Violence and Children draws on the expertise of specialist domestic violence workers and counsellors, psychologists, teachers, mentors and family support workers. It provides essential help and information to all children's service directorates, including professionals in education, social care, health and the voluntary sectors.

Abigail Sterne is a former secondary school teacher and year head and is now an educational psychologist in Oldham, UK.

Liz Poole is a former primary school teacher and is now an educational psychologist in Oldham, UK.

Donna Chadwick works for The Children's Society in Oldham as programme manager. She has developed a specialist counselling service for 4–19 year olds adversely affected by domestic and sexual abuse.

Catherine Lawler works as a therapist, specializing in domestic abuse, she has worked with children, young people and families for 22 years and has a social care background.

Lynda W Dodd is a senior educational and child psychologist in Stockport with responsibility for early intervention and has been an educational psychologist for over 22 years. She is chair of Stockport Women's Aid and Refuge.

Domestic Violence and Children

A handbook for schools and early years settings

Abigail Sterne and Liz Poole
with Donna Chadwick, Catherine Lawler
and Lynda W Dodd

Routledge
Taylor & Francis Group

LONDON AND NEW YORK

First published 2010
by Routledge
2 Park Square, Milton Park, Abingdon, Oxon OX14 4RN

Simultaneously published in the USA and Canada
by Routledge
270 Madison Avenue, New York, NY 10016

Routledge is an imprint of the Taylor & Francis Group, an informa business

© 2010 Abigail Sterne and Liz Poole. Jessica Crawford, illustrations.

Typeset in Garamond by
Pindar NZ, Auckland, New Zealand
Printed and bound in Great Britain by
TJ International Ltd, Padstow, Cornwall

British Library Cataloguing in Publication Data
A catalogue record for this book is available from the British Library

Library of Congress Cataloging-in-Publication Data
Sterne, Abigail.
Domestic Violence and Children: A Handbook for Schools and Early Years
Settings / Abigail Sterne and Liz Poole; with Donna Chadwick, Catherine
Lawler and Lynda Warren Dodd.
    p. cm.
  Includes bibliographical references and index.
  1. Teacher participation in educational counselling—Great Britain.
2. School social work—Great Britain. 3. Abused children—Education—
Great Britain. 4. Child abuse—Great Britain—Prevention. 5. Early
childhood education—Great Britain. I. Poole, Liz. II. Title.
 LB1027.5.S76 2009
    371.7'8—dc22   2009015759

ISBN 10: 0-415-55632-5 (hbk)
ISBN 10: 0-415-46551-6 (pbk)
ISBN 10: 0-203-86910-9 (ebk)

ISBN 13: 978-0-415-55632-3 (hbk)
ISBN 13: 978-0-415-46551-9 (pbk)
ISBN 13: 978-0-203-86910-9 (ebk)

Contents

Foreword

An ambition of the Children's Plan is to make England a better place for children and young people to grow up in. We know that many are privileged to experience genuine personalisation, great teaching and remarkable learning environments where they make progress and thrive. However, there are vulnerable pupils in all our schools who need even more support, understanding and positive interventions if we are to achieve the ambition.

We are one year into the Children's Plan and there is an increasing focus on the attainment of vulnerable groups in school and society. This timely book has brought together a wealth of information and guidance for all those working within Children's Services. It affirms the notion that schools can, and often do, make a difference, especially to the 750,000 children a year who are exposed to domestic violence.

Those who work in schools need to be alert to the many ways that young victims or children of victims communicate, either consciously or unconsciously, that they are living in fear. Persistent absences, high mobility, fatigue, delayed language or cognitive skills, over- or under-reactions to stressful situations are just a few of these. The resulting missed learning opportunities mean that these children fall further and further behind their peers. This book *Domestic Violence and Children* explains in great detail the impact that domestic violence has upon its victims and brings together considerable research in this area. Although the impact is harrowing, later chapters provide realistic guidance and focus on how schools can support families and build resiliency within the young victims.

For the Children's Plan to become a reality and for young people to remain fully engaged with education until at least the age of 18, acquiring the skills, understanding and qualifications that will serve them well in the future, then schools will need the knowledge and skills both to support victims of domestic violence and educate the wider community. *Domestic Violence and Children* provides us with the tools to do this. It is an important book to add to the booklists of education professionals.

Mary Daly
Programme leader for The Inclusion Development Programme
National Strategies

Acknowledgements

In the course of our work, we have had the privilege of meeting and working with dedicated and highly-skilled professionals in women's refuges, family centres, schools and pre-schools. They provide emotional and practical support to children and adults adversely affected by domestic violence. Mothers have attributed their survival to them; young people have spoken of a particular person who has helped them get by.

Our thanks are due to:
Angela Baulk, School Health Adviser
Marion Bunn and Shirley Melia, Pupil Support Centre, Oldham
Nathalie Burke, Oldham Family Crisis Group
Joanne Collier and Pauline Rothwell, The Children's Society, Oldham
Sonia Florent, Parent Partnership, Stockport
Laura Greaves, Tracy Hynes and Andaleeb Saeed, Breeze Hill School, Oldham
Kath Hilton, Beever Primary School, Oldham
Geraldine Hulston, Cedar Mount High School, Manchester
Mike Jones, formerly of St Margaret's CE Primary School, Oldham
Adam Laskey and Heather Woodall, St Thomas CE Primary School, Oldham
Jane Lomax, St Matthew's CE Infants School, Oldham
Nicola Melvin, The Radclyffe School, Oldham
Paula Pollitt and Sandra Almond, Fortalice
Becky Rowe, Connexions
Julie Walker, Holts Family Centre

Thanks are also due to:
The children's refuge workers from the North West Regional Support Workers meetings
Sam Price and all staff, women and children from Stockport Women's Aid
Staff at Rose Bridge High School, Wigan and Plant Hill High School, Manchester
Andrea Derbyshire and staff at the Renaissance Hair and Beauty Salon, Oldham
Davina James-Hanman for her advice and permission to use her work

Our heartfelt appreciation is offered to the mothers, carers and young people who have been willing to share their experiences for the benefit of others.

Special thanks to our family, friends and colleagues for taking the time to read and edit the manuscript and being 'critical friends', including:

David Devane, Safeguarding and Partnerships, Oldham

Everyone at Oldham Educational and Child Psychology Service, particularly Alison Bearn, Debbie Burton, Jayne Grimley and Steve Rooney

Past and present colleagues from Stockport Child and Educational Psychology Service, particularly Alison Wales, Sue McColl, Mark Hancock and Judy Davies

Len Grant, Rob Poole and Geoff Dodd

Michael Sterne

And also to:

Mary Daly, Department for Children, Schools and Families

Peter Farrell, Anne Rushton and Kevin Woods, Manchester University

Christine Williams, formerly of Manchester Educational Psychology Service

Special thanks to:

Joanne Harker, Department for Children, Schools and Families

Susannah Marwood, Women's Aid

Janqui Mehta, Refuge

Sarah Russell, Forced Marriage Unit

We would also like to thank Alison Foyle and Lucy Wainwright of Taylor & Francis, Linda Evans for her original suggestion of a book and Kate Griffiths for encouraging us to write in *Special!* magazine.

Acknowledgements to materials from other publications, web sites or original work:

- The Duluth Wheel (Chapter 1) is reproduced with the following acknowledgement:
  'The Power and Control Wheel was developed by battered women in Duluth who had been abused by their male partners and were attending women's education groups sponsored by the women's shelter. The Wheel used in our curriculum is for men who have used violence against their female partners. While we recognize that there are women who use violence against men, and that there are men and women in same-sex relationships who use violence, this wheel is meant specifically to illustrate men's abusive behaviours toward women. The Equality Wheel was also developed for use with the same curriculum.'
- Women's Aid Federation of England for their definitions of domestic abuse (Chapter 1)
- Refuge: Early Warning Signs poster (Chapter 1)
- Women's Aid Federation of England for permission to include information from http://www.thehideout.org.uk (Chapters 1, 4 and 10)
- Bolton Women's Aid for permission to include a poem from their web site (Chapter 4)
- Cafcass for giving us permission to adapt the matrix, setting out the impact of domestic violence on child development in the Domestic Violence Toolkit, Version 2.1, August 2007 (see Chapters 2 and 3)
- The K.I.D. for his rap (Chapter 10)

- Quotes and references to the work of Davina James-Hanman are reproduced under the terms of the Click-Use Licence (Chapter 13)
- All illustrations are by Jessica Crawford, a student of illustration at Kingston University. She is highly skilled at creating sensitive pictures and is available for commissions. Email: jesscacaca@hotmail.com

Introduction

'Children are very much the silent victims of domestic violence. They may witness it or be subject to it, but often their voice is not heard.'

Home Office 2003: 48

Large numbers of children in our schools and pre-schools live in families where there is domestic violence. It is very common and happens to people from all walks of life: from every social class, race, religion and age group.

A turbulent home environment makes children anxious and unhappy. It can prevent them from thriving in school and learning effectively. It is often a key factor underlying emotional and social difficulties, and problematic behaviour in school, including poor attendance and punctuality.

'My attendance has been poor. I've hardly been in. I've not been so well. I'm worried about my mum. It's just me. I'm too tired, I can't be bothered.'

A teenage girl living in a refuge

Some young people have their education repeatedly disrupted by moving house and changing schools to flee violence. For some, school or pre-school can provide a release from home tensions and a haven of calm; for others, the demands of an educational establishment may add to their anxieties and confusion.

The impact of domestic violence on children often goes unrecognised in education settings. Even when staff know there is something amiss in a family or are aware of the negative impact of domestic violence on a child, they can find it difficult to know what to do and how to safeguard the child and family.

Schools and pre-schools can be hugely beneficial to young people affected by domestic abuse. For many children and families, they are the natural first port of call for help. They provide:

- adults and other young people who can listen and offer support
- help accessing other support services
- a safe and nurturing environment
- consistency, stability and routine for children whose families may be chaotic
- support for parents and carers

- opportunities to learn relationship skills and appropriate ways of dealing with conflict
- opportunities to learn about domestic violence and healthy relationships
- opportunities to develop self-esteem, confidence and resilience.

Many of the ideas for this book come from professionals working in schools with children who experience domestic violence: children's counsellors, family workers, learning mentors, children's refuge workers, teachers and year heads. There are contributions from staff working in schools located near refuges. We also hear from young people and their mothers. Education settings can and do make a real difference to the lives of children from backgrounds of domestic violence but people find this a sensitive and difficult topic. Staff say they need more information and training if they are to feel confident to tackle the issue, support young people and families effectively and educate children about domestic violence. This book aims to address this need.

Part 1 provides background information, key facts, considers the impact of domestic violence on children at different stages of development and the particular issues facing young people living in refuges and temporary accommodation. Domestic violence affects adults' ability to parent effectively so we also consider the impact on mothers.

Part 2 focuses on what schools and early years settings can do to help young people and their families: how they can reach out to parents and ways in which they can support children, including young people in temporary accommodation. There is information about safety and confidentiality, dealing with disclosures and relevant government guidance. Education about domestic violence plays an important role in prevention and we consider ways that schools can teach young people about it.

High quality pastoral care and teaching can provide invaluable support to this vulnerable group of young people. We describe how schools can and do make a difference.

> 'It's about creating an ethos within an organisation. This is what we want to happen within this school. We understand the difficulties that these young people face and although some cause a lot of difficulty in our teaching situation, we have the compassion ... life can throw challenges at you from time to time.'
>
> A head teacher of a primary school near a refuge

A note about male victims of domestic violence

Throughout this book, we generally refer to the abused parent or carer as being female. This should not negate the experiences of male victims of domestic violence; a significant number of men are victims (see key facts about domestic violence, Chapter 1). However, women are more likely to experience sustained or repeated episodes of emotional, physical and psychological abuse, and where domestic violence is known about in schools, it is more likely that staff will be supporting the mother as the abused parent.

We make no distinction when condemning domestic violence, regardless of the victim's sex, age, race or sexuality. It is a basic human right to live life free from the fear of being abused.

The impact of domestic violence on young people and families

Chapter 1

Introduction and background

Children living with domestic violence

Key facts about domestic violence

- One in four women and one in six men will experience domestic violence at some time in their lives. One in nine women are thought to experience domestic violence annually (Council of Europe 2002).
- At least 750,000 children a year in the UK witness domestic violence and nearly three-quarters of children on the 'at risk' register live in households where domestic violence occurs (Department of Health 2002: 16).
- The majority of incidents occur when the children are in the same or the next room (Hughes 1992: 9–11).
- The risk of domestic violence for women is nearly doubled if there are children present in the household (Walby and Allen 2004: 87).
- Seventy per cent of children living in UK refuges have been abused by their father (Bowker *et al.* 1998).
- Thirty per cent of domestic violence starts in pregnancy and between four and nine women in every hundred are abused during their pregnancy and/or after the birth (Department of Health 2005: para 2.4).
- Before a woman reports domestic violence to the police, she will on average have been assaulted 35 times. By the time a woman's injuries are visible, violence is a long-established pattern (Jaffe *et al.* 1986: 38 in Morley and Mullender 1994: 12).
- Violence in teenage relationships is common. More than 40 per cent of young people know girls whose boyfriends have hit them and 40 per cent know girls whose boyfriends have coerced them to have sex (End Violence Against Women 2006: 14–15).
- On average, two women a week are killed by a partner or former partner (Department of Health 2005: para 2.1).

What is domestic violence?

A widely accepted definition, used by the UK government, is: 'any incident of threatening behaviour, violence or abuse (physical, sexual, financial or emotional) between adults who are or have been in a relationship together, or between family members, regardless of gender or sexuality' (Home Office 2005a: 7).

The following is an explanation taken from The Hideout, a web site for young people created by the national domestic violence charity Women's Aid (http://www.thehideout. org.uk). It can be a useful starting point for discussion and teaching.

WHAT IS ABUSE?

Domestic abuse is when one grown-up hurts or bullies another grown-up who is or was their partner, or who is in the same family. Domestic abuse can happen between people who are boyfriend and girlfriend or people who are married.

It can happen when people live together or in different houses. Usually (but not always) it is the man who hurts the woman. Although domestic abuse happens between grown-ups, children can be affected by the abuse that they see and hear. Children can also be hurt or bullied as part of domestic abuse.

Domestic abuse can be:
- *physical* – for example, hitting, pushing, kicking
- *emotional* – sayings things to frighten the other person or make them feel bad
- *sexual* – making someone do sexual things that they don't want to
- *financial* – such as taking away the other person's money, or not letting them get a job.

Domestic abuse is a repeated pattern of behaviour. Grown-ups use domestic abuse to control other people. If someone in your family is abusive, remember it's not your fault. If this is happening in your family, remember that you are not alone. Domestic abuse happens in many families and there are people that can help you and your family. Everyone has the right to be and feel safe.

Reproduced with kind permission of Women's Aid Federation of England

What children see, hear and experience

Around 750,000 children a year are exposed to domestic violence and there will be children affected by it in almost every school (Department of Health 2002: 16). For many, home is a stressful, unpredictable place; the family is a source of conflict and some children live in an almost constant state of fear about the next violent episode. Children may fear for the safety of their mother and themselves. Violent acts are often committed by someone who should be caring for and protecting them. The impact is profound, the fear never goes away and young people can be traumatised by their experiences.

'The force of a shouting adult can feel like a terrible tidal wave to a child.'

Sunderland and Hancock 1999: 35

'Children hear their parents, the adults they love and depend on, screaming in anger, pleading in fear and sobbing in pain. They hear fists hitting bodies, objects thrown and shattered, people thrown against walls and knocked to floors. They may see blood, bruises and weapons. Some children witness domestic rapes.'

Wolak and Finkelhor 1998: 74

One study of children and mothers exposed to domestic violence, found the following (McGee 2000: 66):

- eighty-five per cent of children were present while their mothers were being abused in some way
- in 71 per cent of families, children saw their mothers being physically assaulted
- fifty-eight per cent of children overheard the violence. For example, children were in bed and woke up because of the violence or were sent out of the room
- twenty-seven per cent of children witnessed the outcome of the violence, for example, injury to the mother.

Some parents may think or hope that their children are unaware of the violence or the extent of it; that they may not actually have seen anything. In fact children are usually far more aware than parents like to believe.

Children may hear or witness some of the following:

- verbal abuse, screaming, swearing
- their mothers being grabbed, hit, kicked, beaten, choked – resulting in bruises, cuts, broken bones, lost teeth, internal injuries or miscarriages
- objects being thrown, the use of knives or other weapons
- the outcome of the abuse – the distress, injury to the mother, the mother going to hospital, the police arriving
- windows being smashed, doors kicked down
- parts of their homes and furniture destroyed
- their toys and possessions being damaged or destroyed – favourite toys, comforters may be deliberately destroyed
- their pets being deliberately tortured or killed
- their mothers being sexually assaulted.

'Dad pinned mum up against the stairs. I went for him with a knife. Dad smacked me across the head and my sister got kicked.'

A primary school boy

'When I was nine, my mum got seriously beaten up. I saw every little piece of it. I was really scared and phoned the police. My mum had to go to hospital.'

A primary school girl

Some schools will be aware that a child comes from a home where there is domestic violence, though many children will be living with domestic violence of which schools are unaware. Out of fear and shame, many children make great efforts to hide it from the outside world. Some children and their mothers will have fled domestic violence, though may still live in fear of it and the mother may still be threatened and intimidated by a former partner. Some children suffer the embarrassment of knowing that neighbours and friends have overheard or witnessed incidents and are discussing it. Although frequently the abuse occurs behind closed doors, it can also occur in public.

'The effect of domestic violence on children is such that it must be considered as abuse. Either witnessing it, or being the subject of it is not only traumatic in itself but is likely to adversely impact on a child and it should be treated as physical or emotional abuse as appropriate.'

Department for Education and Skills 2006: 74

The impact on children's well-being and safety

- Children may be woken up by arguments and fighting; they may lie in bed listening.
- Children may get hurt when they try and intervene to protect their mother or siblings.
- Children may be left terrified as to what will happen next.
- After violent episodes, mothers may be physically and emotionally unavailable for their children and unable to tackle basic parenting tasks such as getting the children up and out and providing breakfast.

- Older children may be driven to leaving home.
- Children may have limited access to food, money, clothes and health care (if the abuser controls money and movements).
- Children may live with the fear of having to appear in court as a witness and of their father being imprisoned – for which they could then be blamed.

Some children live like this for most or all of their childhood. The terror can have a profound and lasting impact. Research has shown that the length of time children have been living with domestic abuse has more impact on children's stress levels than the degree or severity of violence (Rossman *et al.* 1994). A range of studies highlights the profound long-term effect (for example McGee 2000: 69).

There will be children in most schools who arrive in the morning or after the weekend in a high state of anxiety about what they have seen or heard. They may be exhausted from lack of sleep. Their stress is ongoing and often heightened by the element of unpredictability characteristic of domestic abuse. Children do not know when the next incident will happen, but they know it will happen, so they are in a continual state of high alert and arousal. They may therefore be over-sensitive to perceived threat, for example, shouting or criticism from adults or other children.

Links with other forms of child abuse

There is a recognised link between domestic violence and child sexual, physical, emotional abuse and neglect. Many violent men who abuse their partners also abuse their children; the overlap is estimated to be between 30 and 66 per cent (Edleson 1999: 134). There can be abuse from both parents. The severity of abuse to a mother is linked to the severity of abuse to children in the home. Threatening to hurt the children can be another way of frightening and controlling the mother.

Domestic abuse rarely exists in isolation from other family difficulties and often co-exists with parental alcohol misuse, drug misuse, mental illness or a learning disability. Clearly the effect on all aspects of children's lives is then even more serious.

The links between domestic violence, child abuse and animal cruelty

Children who are emotionally abused often form very strong attachments to their pets. Abusers may use pets as a tool to control, threaten, intimidate and frighten other family members. They may harm pets or even kill them. Different studies have found that acts of animal abuse are used to coerce, control and intimidate children to remain in, or be silent about, abusive situations (Becker and French 2004). Child sexual abuse survivors have also reported that threats to and abuse of their pets were used to gain control and ensure their silence.

Concern for pets may prevent women and children from leaving violent partners, fearing that if they do, pets may be left to roam, be put down or suffer at the hands of the abuser. This will cause added distress and trauma for the family – particularly for the children, who rely on their pets as a means of comfort in chaotic families. Pet fostering services, such as *Paws for Kids*, can help (see information on web sites and helplines in Chapter 14).

Children's reactions to violence in the home

Children find arguments and violence between adults very disturbing. The charity Childline has reported that many would rather themselves be hit than allow their mothers to be beaten; it is easier to bear the physical pain of being hurt than emotional hurt and feelings of helplessness.

Children will act in different ways in order to try and keep their mother and the rest of the family safe and may put themselves at risk. For example:

- some children know that by entering the room, their parents will stop arguing, as they won't fight in front of the children;
- some children may physically intervene in a fight between parents, and so risk getting hurt;
- some children will try to mediate between parents, or do things to distract them;
- some children will try and get help for their mothers from school or from agencies such as Childline;
- some children will stay out on particular evenings and sleep over at friends' homes to avoid being present during violent incidents;
- some children will go to their rooms and hide or play loud music to drown out the conflict.

'I just go upstairs and turn the telly on in my bedroom – that works for me.'

A primary school pupil during circle time

Who are the abusers?

Abusers come from all walks of life – from all ethnic groups, religions, social classes, age groups and neighbourhoods. Domestic violence can occur in lesbian, gay and bisexual relationships, as well as in heterosexual ones. The majority of abusers are men and the effects of violence are markedly more severe for women. Abusers can be parents, step-parents, in-laws or siblings. Since typically they display different behaviour in public than they do in private, many people are not aware of domestic violence when it is happening in their community. Victims can be too embarrassed or fear they will not be believed if they speak out or try and leave a violent relationship. Sometimes it can be difficult for others to believe that a person who behaves respectably in public can behave appallingly with their family.

'We had a situation … the abuser was an authoritative figure in the local community … at home he was subjecting his wife to horrendous abuse; she had nobody to turn to … she had tried to tell people. Domestic violence does occur anywhere and that situation was incredibly difficult for the children.

This man had a tremendous amount to lose, so was determined to keep control. He portrayed his wife to be mentally unstable; she had worked for years and it was a big deal for her and her children to walk away from her home and possessions. The children had to move from a large house with expensive furnishing and computer games, to sharing a room in the refuge.'

Refuge children's worker

Male victims

Men also experience domestic violence and there are fewer and far less publicised support networks for men. Society does not condemn violence by women against men as much as it does violence by men against women and men can feel stigmatised by it and embarrassed to seek support. It is noted that 'organisations working with men report a high degree of scepticism amongst professionals and the public towards male victims' (House of Commons 2008: 23). Education professionals should be aware that one in six men will experience domestic violence at some time in their lives; fathers can also be victims of domestic violence.

Domestic violence and disabled people

Disabled people and those with learning difficulties are especially vulnerable to abuse. They can face particular barriers in accessing support as the abuser may also be the carer, so the victim may be dependent on the abuser for help with mobility, medication or communication (House of Commons 2008: 25).

'Honour'-based violence

This is a form of domestic violence that can affect young people, and particularly young women, in our schools. It occurs in communities where the concepts of honour and shame are fundamentally bound up with the expected behaviour of families and individuals.

The following are some of the ways in which honour is perceived to be damaged (Brandon and Hafez 2008: 6):

• defying parental authority
• becoming 'western' (clothes, behaviour, attitude)
• women having relationships and sex before marriage
• using drugs or alcohol
• being the subject of gossip.

Victims, including young people in school, can be subject to physical abuse and bullying as punishment for bringing dishonour on the family. 'Honour'-based violence differs in that it is often perpetrated by more than one individual, who can be from the family or wider community (House of Commons 2008: 13).

Forced marriage

> 'A forced marriage is a marriage in which one or both spouses do not (or, in the case of some vulnerable adults, cannot) consent to the marriage and duress is involved. Duress can include physical, psychological, financial, sexual and emotional pressure.'
>
> HM Government 2008: 8

A forced marriage is different to an arranged marriage, where the choice whether or not to respect the arrangement remains with the prospective spouses (House of Commons 2008: 4). Some young people in our schools and colleges are subject to forced marriages and are often taken out of education early. Thirty per cent of the enquiries and cases dealt with by the Government's Forced Marriage Unit concerned under 18s; 15 per cent of these were men (House of Commons 2008: 5). It is likely that many more cases go unreported.

Violence against women from ethnic minorities

Women from ethnic minorities can face particular difficulties when seeking help. These include racism, language barriers, social isolation and immigration status issues. Many know that if they seek help and are found out, they and their children will be ostracised by the community for shaming the family honour and betraying the community. Such women can be subject to abusive and oppressive practices within the family, and domestic violence can include imprisonment within the home, restrictions on lifestyle and freedom of movement and other controlling behaviour (Calder *et al.* 2004: 40).

Women who enter the UK as the spouse of a person settled in the UK are granted limited leave to remain and may have no recourse to public funds; this may mean limited access to temporary or refuge accommodation. These victims of domestic violence are particularly vulnerable; trapped in a pattern of abuse they are unable to leave because their immigration status makes them totally financially dependent on the abuser (House of Commons 2008: 24).

Abuse in teenage relationships

Abuse in teenage relationships is widespread. Many young people feel pressure to be in a relationship; some may tolerate an abusive relationship rather than not have a partner. There have been suggestions that young girls may even regard being hit by their boyfriend as a badge of honour (House of Commons 2008: 32). Young women may find their partner's behaviour confusing. In addition, the abusive male may deliberately isolate a young woman from her friends; she may not know who to talk to or who to turn to for help. A worrying trend is for music and raps to glorify violence, including domestic violence.

Children who abuse parents

Some mothers describe receiving physical and emotional abuse from their children. The underlying motive is likely to be similar to that of adult abusers in domestic violence situations, i.e. to gain power and control over the parent. It can take similar forms to adult domestic abuse and some mothers feel that their child models their behaviour on that of a violent partner:

> 'Because he's seen it, he thinks it's the right thing to do. He thinks if dad can hit mum, I'll do it.'
>
> A mother

The abuse might be verbal, physical or financial, such as demanding or stealing money or incurring debts that the parents will have to take responsibility for. Sometimes it is fuelled by alcohol or drugs. Where schools are aware of this, they should support the mother in seeking help from services such as Child and Adolescent Mental Health Services (CAMHS) or Parentline Plus (see information in Chapter 14 on web sites and helplines).

Characteristics of an abusive home environment

The following are characteristics of oppressive and abusive relationships, which create a home atmosphere of tension and fear.

- The victim suffers threats and intimidation, whether or not the abusive partner is physically present. Use of a mobile phone and email for this is common when the abuser is not there in person.
- The victim is frequently blamed, criticised, undermined, ridiculed or humiliated.
- The abusive partner gives the other little or no authority in the house.
- The victim has their movement outside the home restricted.
- The abuser demonstrates extreme possessiveness and tight monitoring of their partner's behaviour.
- The abuser makes repeated accusations of infidelity.
- The abuser makes threats of divorce and abandonment.
- The abuser takes total control of the household's money.
- The abuser isolates the family from friends, extended family and the community.
- The abusive partner limits the other's contact with school, health professionals and external agencies.
- The abuser makes threats about deportation and return to the country of origin.

> 'We had to sneak downstairs to eat when dad fell asleep.'
>
> A child in a refuge

Domestic violence is often a family secret. Few other adults may come into a child's life, so the child may feel there is no one they can trust or turn to for help; they may fear others' disbelief. Some children learn from a young age that this is not something they should speak about: that it would be a betrayal. They may live in fear of punishment by the abuser or of being taken into care.

> 'This boy is open and not frightened to tell you what's going on. Kids don't always say. They are sworn to secrecy, frightened to tell.'
>
> A pastoral manager

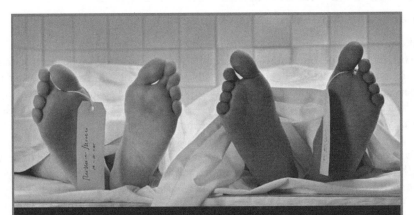

Every week, another two women escape domestic violence.

According to the Home Office, two women in England and Wales are killed by their partner or ex-partner *every week*.

At Refuge, we've learned in our 37 years that what starts as a slap or shove can escalate into a pattern of frequent brutal beatings, and can even lead to death.

We've learned that far from being about *losing control*, domestic violence is actually about men *taking control*.

And we've learned that emotional abuse can do a huge amount of harm.

Forewarned is forearmed, so Refuge would like to alert you to some of the early warning signs of domestic violence.

- Is the man in your life charming one minute and terrifyingly aggressive the next?
- Is he excessively jealous and possessive?
- Is he stopping you from seeing your family and friends?
- Is he constantly criticizing you and putting you down in public?
- Does he control your money?
- Does he tell you what to wear, who to see, where to go, what to think?
- Does he pressure you to have sex when you don't want to?
- Are you starting to walk on eggshells to avoid making him angry?

Refuge

For women and children.
Against domestic violence.

Don't ignore the early warning signs. www.refuge.org.uk

Registered charity no: 277424

Early warning signs

Reproduced with kind permission of Refuge (http://www.refuge.org.uk). Downloadable from the web site.

How and why domestic abuse happens

Verbal abuse and threats in a relationship usually start long before the first violent assault. After this, incidents become more severe and frequent over time. At the heart of domestic abuse lie issues of power and control. The abuser threatens and frightens other family members and commits violent acts so as to impose his will and get his way, ensuring he has complete control. It is an effective way of having the final say in all matters. Tensions in a family will affect the relationships between adults, children and siblings.

> 'I've been on home visits … she's not spoken one word to you … he's done all the talking and there she is, like a frightened rabbit. Or maybe they only give you one contact number and it's his … yet she's not working and is at home all day.'
>
> A family support worker

Duluth Power and Control Wheel

DOMESTIC ABUSE INTERVENTION PROJECT
202 East Superior Street
Duluth, Minnesota 55802
218-722-2781
www.duluth-model.org

The Duluth Domestic Violence Intervention Project (1981) states that physical abuse or violence is never an isolated incident and is only one part of a whole series of behaviours abusers use against their partners. It devised a 'Power and Control Wheel' as a conceptual way of looking at the primary tactics abusers use. This represents the entire system of domestic violence. At the hub is the perpetrator's need to get and keep power and control over his or her partner's life. Each spoke of the wheel represents one of the tactics that may be used to control the victim.

The outer rim of physical and sexual violence surrounds and supports the spokes. It holds the system together and gives it strength.

Abusers' perspectives

Abusers often blame their victims and claim they, the abusers, are provoked to the point where they lose control; they may give the excuse that they have a short fuse and problems managing their anger. Yet researchers and victims point to the fact that abusers are well aware of what they are doing and rather than not being able to control themselves, they are extremely controlling. Young people have described an abuser's enjoyment in knowing he can get away with it. Drink and drugs can act as disinhibitors to abusers and many women and children have described their dread of their partner or a parent coming in drunk or drug fuelled. Sometimes, when there is a regular pattern, children may plan to sleep elsewhere.

The continued risks to women and children during and after separation

Often a woman is most vulnerable to extreme violence at the point of separation, when her partner realises he is losing control of her. Mothers and children who have left violent men continue to be at risk, as harassment can continue long afterwards, so the stress continues. Even when they move to a secret new address, they often live in fear of being found and of the violence beginning again. Further incidences of threats, abuse and assault often occur around contact arrangements, so for children these times can be highly charged. Children suffer because the abuser:

- uses the opportunity of contact to discharge anger and frustration
- uses contact as an opportunity to blame the mother, saying the family would still be together if the mother had been reasonable, thus causing division between her and her children
- uses contact visits to exert control over the mother's movements
- may be unreliable and unpredictable
- says or does things to get back at the mother.

A cycle of violence in families?

Domestic violence gives children poor models of relationships; some may grow up with the idea that hitting within families is normal. However, it is important not to make the assumption that young people who experience domestic violence will automatically go on to be perpetrators or victims, thus continuing the so-called 'cycle of violence'. School staff can help these young people understand that there is no inevitability to them becoming violent adults or victims of domestic abuse; staff can challenge labels and stereotypes that may become attached to children (see further Chapter 10).

Risk and resilience in children and young people

Children and young people will respond to situations of extreme stress – whether long-term or brief – in different ways. Some seem able to cope with apparently unbearable situations, while others cannot.

Resilience factors in children include:

- having a parent (usually the mother) who can maintain reasonable parenting skills whilst dealing with the domestic violence
- the mother responding confidently to challenging situations and therefore providing a positive role model
- the mother being mentally healthy, i.e. not suffering from anxiety or depression related to the abuse
- the mother being perceived by the children as continuing to be able to support and care for them
- having people they can turn to (perhaps someone on the school staff, or a counsellor) for emotional support when needed
- having strong support networks, e.g. friends, children, siblings, other supportive family members.

Humphreys 2006

Risk factors for children include:

- long-term exposure to domestic violence, perhaps where the mother has experienced it with a number of partners
- witnessing traumatic events such as physical or sexual assault on the mother by a violent partner or ex-partner
- being the victim of other forms of child abuse
- experiencing homelessness or frequent changes of home, possibly in and out of refuges and temporary accommodation or living with relatives in over-crowded situations
- frequent changes of school – disrupting education and reducing the chances of establishing long-standing relationships with other pupils and adults
- living in poverty.

'These children think they don't count.'

Primary school learning mentor

The importance of supportive staff in pre-schools and schools

Staff in early years settings and schools are well placed to make a positive difference to the lives of young people and to increase their resilience. Doyle (2003), writing about emotionally abused children, described how even one teacher involved for a limited time could make an inestimable contribution to the constructive survival of the victims of emotional abuse. Mullender *et al.* (2002: 219) found that informal supports topped children's lists of what helped them, with specialist domestic violence services next:

> 'this is not the same as becoming social workers … It means being an effective channel for children to gain access to welfare services outside the school, by opening up an early opportunity for them to confide that something is wrong. Children would like to go to their teachers as a route to getting help for themselves and their mothers.'

Staff may feel there are significant barriers to their being able to help; for example, large classes with limited opportunities for individual contact or a lack of training on this issue. Also, children who have experienced domestic violence can present behaviour that is challenging to even the most skilled and experienced staff. In later chapters, we discuss strategies to overcome some of these barriers, address the challenges, support pupils' resilience and develop self-esteem. Many schools offer quality support to these vulnerable pupils.

Domestic violence poses significant risks to children's physical and mental health and has an adverse effect on their well-being. The key message throughout this book will be that although staff in schools may not be able to stop the violence at home, they are in a position to make a considerable difference to children's lives.

We will now examine in more detail the psychological impact of domestic violence on mothers and their children.

Chapter 2

The impact on babies and young children

'Events in early life, especially those experienced with strong emotion, can and do remain an influence throughout our lives and are difficult to erase. Early experienced precognitive emotions continue to play out in later life even though the individual may have no conscious memory of the association.'

LeDoux 1996: 85

Domestic violence, pregnancy and the impact on under 5s

Domestic violence often begins during pregnancy and presents considerable risks to women and their unborn children. Babies and very young children can suffer considerably as a result. The effects may include:

- death of the baby due to premature labour, miscarriage or forced termination
- poor foetal growth and consequent effects on brain development
- difficulties in developing secure attachments
- eating difficulties and, in extreme cases, failure to thrive
- behavioural difficulties – anger, aggression and impulsivity; a more extreme startle response or, conversely, quiet, passive and less responsive behaviours
- emotional distress such as clinginess, restlessness, irritability, nervousness and crying
- problems with socialising and sharing
- distress and confusion
- fear of new people and situations; fear of the perpetrator
- developmental regression (especially in toileting and language)
- sleep disturbances, including nightmares.

Refuge, a domestic violence charity for women and children, highlights the over-representation of children under five years of age growing up in homes where domestic violence occurs, and the paucity of services that exist to support this group (Refuge 2005). It describes babies and very young children as a 'significant and challenging group' because:

- they are at risk of being injured by domestic violence incidents due to their closeness to and dependence on their mothers. They may be held as a shield by the mother, hit by thrown objects, or intentionally threatened or hurt to terrify the mother;
- they are more likely to be overwhelmed by exposure to violence. Even when apparently lying passively in their cots or pushchairs, infants are extremely sensitive to their surroundings and especially to the emotional signals given out by their caregiver – depression, anxiety, anger, fear;
- they are less able to make sense of and communicate with anyone about their violent experiences;
- they themselves are at risk of being abused or severely neglected;
- there are lasting consequences for a child's development.

Levendosky *et al.* (2002) found that pre-school children who witness domestic violence or live in families where domestic violence occurs suffer from symptoms of Post-Traumatic Stress Disorder (PTSD; for more detail, see Chapter 3). This age group seemed 'most vulnerable to symptoms of re-experiencing the trauma and hyperarousal' (p. 159).

Domestic violence and early brain development

Domestic violence can affect early brain development (Glaser 2000). At birth, a baby's brain is 25 per cent of its adult weight. By the end of the first year it has increased to 66 per cent of its adult weight because of the 'brain growth spurt' that occurs between the seventh pre-natal month and the child's first birthday. The developing brain is most vulnerable to the impact of traumatic experiences during this time. In addition, during the first three years of life, the human brain is laying down neural pathways, which are influenced by exposure to extreme trauma. This will change the organisation of the brain, resulting in difficulties in dealing with stresses in later life (Perry 1997).

So even before birth, early emotional trauma such as domestic violence directly affects the development of a baby's brain. When humans suffer stress, levels of the steroid hormone cortisol rise. However, cortisol has a toxic effect on newly-formed brain cells. Raised levels of cortisol during pregnancy can result in poor foetal growth and can affect brain development (Quinlivan 2000). It is as if these babies have been primed to be reactive and are 'hypervigilant' – always on the look-out for danger.

If young children are exposed to domestic violence and the associated stress, they may continue to display hypervigilance and hyperarousal, the 'fight or flight' response, at nursery and school. However it must be recognised that this pattern of behaviour can serve as a protection for children living with violence. Children may be inclined to aggression and may display characteristics such as difficulties focusing on an activity and being over active.

In contrast the young child may react with a different evolutionary response, 'freeze and surrender', whereby the child is unreactive and dissociated. This can develop into 'frozen watchfulness' in older children. Davies (1999: 118) refers to this as 'hyperalertness, hyperarousal and numbing'. Schore (2001) reports that emotional neglect or trauma very early in life can often lead to the impairment of brain-mediated functions such as empathy and attachment, and can affect the regulation of emotions.

Disrupted early attachments

Babies' attachments to their caregivers are disrupted by exposure to domestic violence (Gerhardt 2004). The more serious the levels of domestic violence are, the higher the likelihood of insecure attachments. The attachment figure, usually the mother, can be a source of both fear and comfort. Babies are both afraid *of* and *for* their mothers. In these confusing circumstances, the baby does not develop a consistent or coherent strategy for obtaining help and comfort from its mother.

Confusion, distress and the impact on infant behaviour

Infants find it very difficult to make sense of the violence they have witnessed or experienced. No one can explain what is happening; the mother's sense of helplessness can lead her to dissociate from the violence and act as if there is nothing wrong. The child's thoughts and feelings about the experience become fragmented, disorganised and incomprehensible (McIntosh 2002). Younger children generally do not have the ability to express their feelings verbally, so they communicate through their behaviour. By three years old, children exposed to domestic violence generally show heightened levels of distress and aggression.

It is vital that professionals are aware that young children who are abused by their parents, or who witness abuse, can present as quiet, well-behaved and smiley. These are adaptive safety behaviours that mask underlying fear. Children's observable reactions to the violence may not tally with their emotional reactions. It may take some time before children are able to show any reaction at all. This does not mean that the child is unaffected.

Feelings of insecurity, anxiety and self-blame

The dangerous circumstances of home life may leave children insecure and lacking trust in adults. They usually do not understand the reasons for the abuse and think they must have done something wrong. Self-blame can precipitate feelings of guilt, worry and anxiety. Young children experience great stress when they have no consistent or secure environment.

Delayed language and cognitive development

Children from backgrounds of domestic violence are more likely to have delayed language and cognitive development. Reasons for this include:

- A mother who is anxious and depressed is less likely to interact as much verbally, play and provide stimulating activities for her infant at a time that is crucial for a child's language development.
- A home atmosphere of fear and unpredictability is not conducive to imitating and trying out new sounds and words. As a coping strategy, young children may learn to be still and quiet.

Refuge 2005

Summary of possible indicators of domestic violence: Foundation Stage

Psychological/ emotional	Difficulty in separating from the main carer; anxiety; excess crying; clingy, insecure behaviour; startled response to noise or unexpected approaches; tantrums with excessive strong language and aggression; passivity and a lack of interest in surrounding activity; defensive behaviours with toys or food
Social	Poor communication skills; difficulties relating to other children, poorly developed play skills, avoidant behaviour; possessiveness with toys, difficulties sharing; aggressive behaviour beyond the norm, or withdrawn behaviour
Physical	Unkempt, tired, hungry, delayed toileting; parent having difficulty keeping appointments, so delayed identification of hearing/visual or physical problems; signs of physical abuse (past or present)
Learning	Language delay; delayed play skills and progress across early learning goals
Resilience factors	Nurturing care; support for the abused parent; a responsive key worker; someone to help the parent monitor and keep medical appointments; adult structured play opportunities that model and foster social and emotional development

NB This table sets out some common responses to domestic violence but children differ in their responses and may display symptoms at any stage so the suggested signs are not 'fixed'; some children display more resilience than others. There can be many reasons why worrying indicators are present – domestic violence is one possibility. In some circumstances Common Assessment Framework or child protection procedures may be needed – this is true across all key stages. With acknowledgement to Cafcass (August 2007).

Summary

Babies and very young children are deeply and traumatically affected by domestic violence, and the impact can be long term. Research contradicts commonly-held beliefs that they are too young to notice or understand. In Chapter 9, we will consider how early years settings can play a crucial role in the lives of very young children who have experienced domestic violence.

Chapter 3

The impact on school-aged children

'There may be serious effects on children who witness domestic violence, which often result in behavioural issues, absenteeism, ill health, bullying, anti-social behaviour, drug and alcohol mis-use, self-harm and psycho-social impacts.'

HM Government 2006: 202

'It is very difficult for children and young people to fully engage in and benefit from education when they have an insecure base, when they feel fearful, anxious and uncertain, when they feel helpless, when their mother is possibly disorganised, depressed and even neglectful.'

A refuge worker quoted in Mill and Church 2006: 9

Introduction

Chapter 2 described how domestic violence affects brain development in very young children, the emotional impact on infants and the possible longer-term effects. We now look at the range of impacts on school-aged children.

Domestic abuse causes great distress and anxiety to children and affects their lives and their education in many ways. Every set of circumstances is unique, but children from families where there has been severe or prolonged domestic violence are much more likely to develop challenging behaviour, emotional and social difficulties. These may continue for a long time after the traumatic events have occurred.

In school, children may display:

- externalising behaviour: hostility, anger outbursts, aggression, oppositional behaviour
- internalising behaviour: shyness, being withdrawn, passive behaviour, depression, anxiety, low self-esteem.

Domestic violence may also impact negatively on:

- attention and concentration skills
- cognitive skills
- language development
- school attainments

- attendance and punctuality
- social development.

Different factors will influence how and to what extent children are affected, and the longer-term impact. These include:

- the age and developmental level of the child
- the length of time child has been exposed to domestic violence. For some, this will be his or her entire life
- the nature of the abuse and the levels of fear experienced. The child will worry greatly about the mother's well-being and safety. Living in fear long term has a profound effect
- the relationship with the abuser, e.g. parent, step-parent, brother
- the effect on the mother's mental health and ability to parent effectively.

It should also be noted that some children who live with domestic abuse achieve highly in school; throwing themselves into school life and work can provide an escape. Yet in terms of emotional development, they are unlikely to emerge unscathed.

In *Promoting Children's Mental Health within Early Years and School Settings* (Department for Education and Employment 2001: 8), three factors in children's and young people's lives are identified that can result in them being at increased risk of developing mental health difficulties; these include:

- loss or separation – including resulting from parental separation, divorce or hospi-talisation, loss of friendships especially in adolescence, family breakdown that results in the child having to live elsewhere;
- life changes – including moving house, changing schools;
- traumatic events – including abuse and violence.

Many children who live with domestic abuse experience all of these.

The psychological impact

Children who live in fear

Children who live with domestic violence live with high and sometimes unbearable levels of fear and insecurity. They may arrive at school tense; hating having to leave their mothers in the morning; there may have been resistance or tantrums. They may be anxious during the day, dreading what will happen when they get home. Yet frightened children do not always present as such in school, and the fear that underlies emotional and behavioural difficulties can go unrecognised. Arguably, this is the most common and pernicious form of child emotional abuse.

> 'Most of us can go home at the end of a day and relax and unwind; for these children there's no let up. I've taken children home and they have sneaked in the house and they just don't want to be noticed. They just want peace.'
>
> A family support worker

Children living with domestic violence may fear:

- injury or death to their mother
- disputes and violence happening while they are at school
- the stress and toll that the violence takes on their mother
- for the safety and well-being of other family members such as siblings, or of their pets
- injury to themselves
- damage to their home or possessions
- the police intervening in disputes; the embarrassment of neighbours and friends hearing or seeing the violence
- family separation
- being uprooted; having to leave their home, possessions, pets
- arguments about contact visits – centred on them
- punishment and other consequences of telling someone
- social services getting involved; being removed from their family.

'You just want to go home and be with your mum. Make sure she's OK. Make things calm. You think is your mum all right? Are they arguing right now? What's happening?'

A secondary school girl

'Young people are often withdrawn and worrying inwardly. Children worry about leaving mum. They feel they protect each other and need reassurance.'

A school attendance officer

'Normally my dad walks out and threatens things; sometimes he will do them.'

A primary school girl

'One teacher told the head teacher and she told social services. There was no need for that. I was upset and got into trouble from my mum.'

A secondary school girl

Note that it is often difficult for staff to reconcile the wishes of the child with their responsibility for safeguarding children. Professionals have a duty to prioritise safeguarding.

A child whose family has fled domestic violence may worry about:

- the continued threat of harm to their mother or themselves
- being tracked down by the abuser
- being abducted
- pending court cases and residency decisions
- contact with a non-resident parent
- the dark, nightmares, loud noises

- the threat of damage to their home or possessions
- feelings that they are 'going mad' because of past traumatic events
- the financial implications of family separation
- the well-being of the pets they have left behind.

'I'm scared that my dad will find me and kidnap me. My mum saw him near where we live. I worry about getting off a bus. He has a car and could drive past. He knows where we are.'

A secondary school girl

'My son has always been so scared of finding me dead. He always told me how much he loved and missed me. It certainly affected his learning and behaviour.'

A mother

'Another thing that came up during counselling; he was worrying about how Christmas would go, now that dad was no longer living with us.'

A mother

'I'm not sure if I'm going on the class trip. My mum's gone, but she's still getting all the benefits. My dad's got no money.'

A primary school boy

Some children will have enjoyed a positive relationship with the abuser, while at the same time wanting the abuse to stop. They may grieve the loss of a resident parent and be confused by their ambivalent feelings.

Domestic violence and trauma

A number of studies (Pynoos and Eth 1986; Kilpatrick *et al.* 1997; Lehmann, 1997) state that many children witnessing domestic violence meet the clinical criteria for Post-Traumatic Stress Disorder (PTSD); a severe anxiety disorder following a traumatic event or a succession of traumatic events. What is particularly difficult for children living with domestic violence is the fact that the trauma occurs within the family and the perpetrator, as parent, may be someone they love and who should be protecting them from harm. The violence takes place in the home, which should be a safe haven. The impact on children has been compared to that observed in children living in war zones.

Symptoms of post-traumatic stress in children include:

- repetitive dreams and nightmares
- flashbacks
- joyless play
- a feeling of going mad
- over-activity and irritability
- impaired concentration and memory
- bed-wetting and soiling
- self-abuse.

Terr 1991: 10–20

PTSD will affect every aspect of school life; it can prevent children from learning effectively, participating fully, deriving enjoyment, achieving their potential, behaving appropriately and establishing positive social relationships. Some children have said that they thought there was something wrong with their brains; that they might be insane or schizophrenic.

> 'I have pictures in my head. ... I see it happening over and over again. I was brought up with violence. What do you do if you can't get the picture out of your head?'
>
> A secondary school boy

> 'Hearing voices inside my head; people shouting. I told the doctor and he says I'm not bonkers.'
>
> A primary school boy

> 'He bangs his head on the table. ... He talks of strange things that have happened at home. He gets confused.'
>
> A head teacher

Traumatic memories

Children can be tormented by painful and frightening memories of violence long after it has happened. Events can become blurred and some children may find it difficult to make sense of the timescale. They may give rambling accounts; these can tip into fiction, which can be difficult to distinguish from reality. Children may say things that sound muddled or fantastical and they may be described as prone to lying and exaggeration, though there may be nothing intentionally misleading about their accounts. Some children will fantasise about revenge plans and hurting or killing the abuser. This can be a coping mechanism, reflecting ongoing distress. These young people may be more susceptible to self-harming behaviour and suicidal feelings as they grow up.

> 'I can remember everything when I was a baby. I hid in the shed when dad battered mum ... I'm not allowed to talk about it ... He booted my mum and she tried to run away. I got hit for trying to stop him. My sister and me had to take the knife out ... when I was little, mum and dad used to argue every night.'
>
> A secondary school boy

> 'He won't forget or stop talking about the things he's seen. He repeats exactly what his dad said. It may stay dormant then he reminds me of when I was pinned in a chair with a knife.'
>
> A mother

The pressures to keep the abuse a secret

Many children think domestic violence must remain a family secret. This may be out of shame and embarrassment, out of fear of the abuser, of splitting the family, or of social services intervening and removing them. Quite young children soon learn that domestic abuse is not something openly discussed. They may lie to teachers, other professionals, extended family or friends to conceal the violence.

> 'When things are out in the open, you'll say why didn't you say anything was happening? The reason is fear. They are scared and they are protecting their mums.'
>
> A family support worker

Feelings of responsibility, guilt, self-blame and confusion

Children often feel that they take some blame for the violence and even that they may be an underlying cause of conflict and therefore of violence: maybe their bad behaviour has driven a parent to violence; maybe they are a financial burden; maybe they have caused arguments about discipline or have made excessive demands for time and attention. Children from mixed-race relationships may suffer the additional problem of not knowing which parent to identify with (Hester *et al.* 2000: 76).

These feelings are an enormous burden for children. They may feel they should try and stop the violence occurring and many intervene either verbally or physically. In so doing, they can put themselves in danger.

Shame and embarrassment

Many young people feel ashamed or embarrassed about family violence and dread others knowing about it. They fear neighbours hearing shouting, or parents arguing in front of friends. One girl described how neighbours watched as furniture was flung through windows; then the police and ambulances arrived.

Young people from some minority ethnic communities may be afraid of bringing shame on their family honour if others find out about the domestic violence.

The impact on social relationships

Domestic violence can adversely affect children's relationships with their peers. Some will deliberately distance themselves, fearing their friends knowing about their family situation. Children who constantly worry about home life may feel inhibited and appear guarded or passive. Other children may talk about home with their friends and invite them round to play, but that is difficult for children living in violent homes. They may choose not to have friends round to the house because of family volatility and unpredictability. Children who frequently move house and school may be unwilling to invest in new friendships.

> 'Children, especially boys, don't want people to know that their dad's like that.'
>
> A family support worker

On the other hand, some young people can be overly clingy, possessive, insecure and suffer an underlying fear of further loss. They may be controlling in their relationships with other children or with adults, wanting to be in charge and may have difficulty working or playing to another's agenda. Some may find it difficult to maintain friendships.

> 'She's very possessive about her friends. Once she's formed a bond, she hates it to be threatened. With me too. If I have company, she won't leave me alone.'
>
> A mother

Speech, language and learning delay or difficulties

We have described how young children who have lived with domestic violence may have delayed speech and language development and cognitive skills. This can be because an abused mother is less able to interact and play with her children. A withdrawn, passive or anxious child may spend far less time communicating and developing language and thinking skills than other children. A high level of distress can make a child less able to engage with learning, concentrate and take in new information. In addition, periods of absence from school mean missed learning opportunities and gaps in learning.

Domestic violence and challenging behaviour

Research suggests that around 40 per cent of children who have experienced domestic violence show clinically significant behavioural problems (Holden *et al.* 1998 in Calder 2004: 56).

> 'Watching them fight makes you more aggressive. You might be sat down and refuse to work, so you get out of your seat and wander off. You don't want to be there. When people wind me up, I take it out on others.'
>
> A secondary school girl

'His father was violent and we both took drugs. He saw it, heard it and was scared. He was very aggressive towards people.'

A mother

'There can be verbal abuse and physical aggression; for example, he was banging his friend's head on the table. He finds it difficult to see how problematic his behaviour is.'

A learning mentor

When traumatised children are in stressful situations at school they can become agitated quickly and appear to over-react. Teachers often remark how difficult it is to identify any particular trigger to a behaviour outburst; an innocuous comment may touch a raw nerve; a seemingly minor incident may provoke stress or panic. For example, a child might not have heard the teacher's instructions so cannot start their work; might be stuck; over-react to a negative comment from a peer; or be thrown by a change of routine.

Some children may respond to threatening or stressful situations by going into 'fight' mode and become aggressive and hostile; others may take flight and run out of a lesson or out of school.

'before you know it, they've run off. I'm out in my car trying to find them. You get them back in and they're extremely upset, they're vulnerable, they're crying, they're sorry, but they've just seen red and they've gone off on one. So sympathy please! The kids need somebody to be there, to acknowledge what they've been through and what they are going through and that they're trying.'

A family support worker

These children may be particularly sensitive to shouting, angry adult interactions and to physical contact. They are more likely than other children to interpret their teachers and peers as having hostile intent. They may complain about receiving dirty looks or being picked on. They may be particularly sensitive about verbal abuse directed towards their mothers, as they feel protective; beware of the trend among young people for name-calling directed at mothers.

Beneath the rage, it is frightening for children to feel so out of control. After an outburst, the child can feel terrible – shame, embarrassment and feelings of having let themselves and those who help them down.

There can be severe consequences in school for children who have difficulties containing their anger, including exclusion from lessons and fixed-term or permanent exclusion. Severe behaviour outbursts are indicators of unbearable levels of tension.

A negative model of conflict resolution

Domestic violence provides children with a negative model of how arguments are resolved. Children observe that threats, screaming, swearing and fighting are effective means of exerting control; that one person can frighten another into letting them have their way. They see power imbalances between men and women. Therefore in school, children may also resort to aggressive means:

'This kid has a reputation round school of being volatile; she will kick off at the slightest thing. She points in people's faces and that's what mum's ex-partner used to do to mum.'

A family support worker

Attention and concentration difficulties

It can be difficult for children who are living in fear to concentrate in school. Their preoccupation with safety and security can be a source of concentration difficulties.

'Your work stops. Everything goes out of the window apart from what you're thinking. With it all in your mind, you can't do as well as you know you could.'

A secondary school girl

'He was always so terrified of dad coming to get him. He couldn't learn ... he couldn't concentrate, not even on watching TV.'

A mother

'I'm always questioning these AD/HD diagnoses. Actually, the way they act is normal for what they are experiencing.'

A domestic violence children's counsellor

'He always needs chivvying and effort is erratic. To get anything out of him, you have to sit with him. He finds it difficult to focus.'

A head teacher

Children on high alert

Traumatised children with long-term anxieties may seem to be in a continual state of high arousal. Teachers will be familiar with the child who cannot keep still; who may be fiddling, rocking on their chair, turning round and out of their seat. Some children behave impulsively: shouting out, poking others, lashing out or destroying their work.

Some children grow up with the core beliefs 'I am never safe' and 'I must always be on my guard'. They may be 'hypervigilant', continually scanning the class, distracted from their work. Some may crave adult attention and behave so as to get it; negative attention being better than no attention. These children can be wearing for staff, and their behaviour impacts heavily on their learning and that of others.

> 'Children can blow at anything that triggers an emotional response. They are "lighthouse children". It's as if they put little beacons out and are waiting for the next thing.'
>
> A primary learning mentor

> 'You can't be safe anywhere.'
>
> A secondary school boy

A lack of trust and fear of authority figures

A child who has found adults to be unreliable or untrustworthy may have difficulties trusting school staff. Some children may have observed that authority figures such as a controlling father or older brother, the police or a social worker can do sudden and drastic things. Some may have developed core beliefs that people in authority are to be feared.

'Such a lot had happened; so many adults had let her down. She could not trust adults.'

A mother

Inconsistent parenting

Parenting can be inconsistent if one parent is depressed and oppressed, living under a regime where the other adult dictates the rules. It will be difficult to impose consistent discipline, and behaviour boundaries may be unclear.

Where a mother and her children have moved away from the perpetrator, the family dynamics can change completely. If the father was the disciplinarian and the mother had little authority, she may subsequently struggle to impose her own boundaries. A family support worker noticed that some children seem to 'go off the rails' in school when they no longer live with the abuser and are no longer in fear:

'I think ... while they're in that environment ... the kids learn to keep a lid on things. Nobody's to know. They're scared of mum getting hurt even more. It's only after that person's gone, then it all comes out ... it's like the lid's come off. And that's when we see all this behaviour.'

A family support worker

'All the time, he'd been acting grown up. When his dad left, he took up the role of the man of the family. Now that things are settled, it's as if he's going back to being the little boy again. He shows off, acts the clown at school.'

A mother

Dissociation

Some children cope with overwhelming feelings by dissociating; this is a protective response, where, unconsciously, children temporarily shut down or disengage from their environment so they do not have to feel hurt any more. In school, children who dissociate may present as being in their own world, unresponsive to unpleasant things that are happening around them.

Fatigue and sleep difficulties

Some children may be prevented from sleeping by arguments and fighting or woken by them. Children who are anxious often do not sleep well and their sleep may be disrupted by nightmares. Fatigue has an obvious impact on learning and behaviour.

Separation anxiety

Young children may be excessively clingy and reluctant to separate from their mothers in the morning. They may be very challenging when getting ready for school and use extreme delaying tactics, such as running away or wetting themselves – this can also be an anxiety response. They may arrive at school in a tense and anxious state.

Depressed, passive or withdrawn behaviour

Some children from backgrounds of domestic abuse, in particular those who feel threatened by their parents' violent disputes, may present as quiet, shy and avoidant. It may not be obvious to school staff that they are showing signs of depression.

Children missing education

Many of the above difficulties will affect a child's capacity to learn. The following are other reasons why children from backgrounds of domestic abuse miss out on education.

House moves and changes of school

Some mothers and children move house, some repeatedly, to escape violent or abusive partners. This may involve several changes of school. Finding new school places can be problematic and time consuming, especially secondary placements or placements in the same school for two or more siblings. Children may miss out on weeks or even months of education.

Once in a new school, it can take time to assess a child and it can be difficult to get information from previous schools, especially where there has been a rapid succession of changes. This means there can be delay in implementing appropriate interventions, e.g. in literacy and numeracy. There can be particular difficulties implementing appropriate programmes of support where a child has complex needs or a statement of educational needs as it can be hard for schools to find additional support staff at short notice.

Poor attendance and school refusal

Many children who live with domestic violence are reluctant to attend school. Often they have valid reasons for wanting to stay at home, related to their concern for their mother's safety and well-being. They may feel she is in danger from the abuser, or in need of their emotional support. By staying nearby, children retain peace of mind. Children may also therefore behave so as to get sent home; this could be by feigning illness or being disruptive.

Children as carers

Domestic violence can severely undermine a mother's ability to parent. Some rely on their children for emotional and practical support; older children may take on the role of carer both of their mother and younger siblings. Some girls, in particular, have a considerable burden of responsibilities so feel they need to stay off school. They see that their mother needs practical help and emotional support. One mother described this role reversal and her reliance on her daughter: 'She gets through things. She always tries to be there for me. I do things for her too.'

Summary

Domestic violence has a wide-ranging impact on children's development and emotional well-being; it can affect their whole education. Children who live with the high levels of anxiety induced by domestic violence are unlikely to achieve their educational potential or be content in school.

Domestic violence impacts negatively on children's:

- emotional development
- behaviour
- ability to concentrate and learn effectively
- language and cognitive development
- friendships
- trust in adults
- attendance and punctuality at school
- attainments.

In Part 2, we consider how schools can address some of these negative effects on young people, and support them and their families.

Table 3.1 Indicators of domestic violence at different Key Stages

Possible indicators of domestic violence: Key Stages 1 and 2

Psychological/ emotional	Separation anxiety; clingy, insecure behaviour; easily upset; low self-esteem; preoccupied; intolerance of praise; frequent need for reassurance; fear of authority figures
	Distress that may include: anger, aggression, anxiety, sadness; fear of failure; apparent difficulties distinguishing fact from fantasy; conversely, passive and withdrawn behaviour; dissociation
Social	Difficulties relating to other children; social isolation; aggressive play; bullying or being a victim of bullying; inappropriate attachment to unfamiliar people; a strong sense of justice; sensitivity about being seen as or treated differently to others; children taking on a parenting role
Behavioural	Poor attention and concentration; hyperactivity and hypervigilance; attention-seeking behaviour; challenging behaviour; erratic behaviour; obstructive behaviour motivated by the desire to avoid work or be sent home; inflexibility and a heightened need for control; extreme responses to seemingly minor things; (increasing with age) disaffection; challenging to authority figures
Physical	Unkempt appearance; fatigue; bed-wetting and enuresis; signs of physical injury; hunger; stomach aches, headaches and somatic problems
Learning and play	Delayed language and cognitive skills; poor communication skills; poor cooperative play and turn taking skills; reluctance to try new things; signs of missed early play and learning opportunities; an inconsistent and erratic approach to work; difficulties with group work; destroying work; homework and/or reading at home not done; (increasing with age) underachievement; blocks to learning and failure to progress; work related anxiety; conversely, some children are totally absorbed by schoolwork
School related/other difficulties	Frequent demands to go home; poor attendance or punctuality; frequent changes of school; missed medical appointments
Resilience factors	Support from school for the abused parent; sympathetic, empathetic and vigilant teachers; access to a key, empathetic and supportive member of staff, e.g. a family support worker or learning mentor; opportunities to talk about problems at home as well as for problem free talk; regular school attendance; breakfast clubs; fun activities; belonging to after school and homework clubs; supportive older siblings; supportive wider social networks, having a friend/s; ability to detach from home stresses; attendance at medical appointments; (for older children) help with safety planning; access to counselling services; some flexibility in school rules and adult expectations

Possible indicators of domestic violence: Key Stage 3

Psychological/ emotional	(See also Key Stages 1 and 2) Diminishing self-esteem and feelings of self-worth; depression; conflict over identity; behaviour outbursts, aggression

Social/ behavioural	(See also Key Stages 1 and 2). Young people, especially girls, taking on the role of carer; drawn to groups that indulge in anti-social behaviour, including drinking, taking drugs and criminal activity; lack of sleep; early sexual activity; running away from home; truancy and disaffection with education
Physical	Fatigue; hunger; frequent complaints about illness / being unfit to be in school; unkempt appearance; possible undiagnosed medical conditions because of missed appointments
Learning	Underachievement and disaffection with learning; gaps in learning because of missed opportunities; low attainments; poor attention and concentration; disorganisation and lack of equipment; homework not done; conversely, some children lose themselves in their work
School related/other difficulties	Frequent demands to go home; poor attendance and punctuality; frequent changes of school; missed medical appointments
Resilience factors	(See also Key Stages 1 and 2); a positive relationship with a key adult, e.g. a learning mentor; opportunities to be listened to and for joint problem-solving; learning and behaviour support; some flexibility in school rules and adult expectations; support with personal organisation; ability to separate from the stresses of home; extra-curricular activities, homework clubs; information about sexual health and relationships; support with safety planning; access to counselling services; good friends

Possible indicators of domestic violence: Key Stage 4 and beyond

Psychological/ emotional	(See also Key Stage 3) Self-blame; anxiety about repeating the cycle of violence; anxiety about family, even after leaving home; depression, self-harm and suicidal thoughts, particularly if sexually or physically abused
Social/ behavioural	(See also Key Stage 3) Poor social networks and social skills; use of violence and aggression to solve problems; risk-taking behaviour; anti-social behaviour; criminal behaviour
Physical	(See also Key Stage 3) Risk of pregnancy or sexually transmitted disease; missed medical/dental appointments; health problems may be related to drug and alcohol abuse
Learning	(See also Key Stage 3) Excluded or not attending school
Resilience factors	(See also Key Stage 3) 'Access to an adult who acts as a champion, committed to the young person and acting vigorously and persistently on their behalf' (Cafcass Domestic Violence Toolkit Version 2.1, August 2007); a professional who can understand about caring responsibilities; ambitions and future plans and support to achieve these

NB. Children differ in their responses to domestic violence. These tables set out some possible indicators, though these may of course signal other difficulties. The signs are not 'fixed' and some children display more resilience than others. In some circumstances, it may be appropriate to start Common Assessment Framework (CAF) or Child Protection (CP) procedures – this is true across all key stages.

With acknowledgement to Cafcass Domestic Violence Toolkit, VERSION 2.1, August 2007

Chapter 4

Families in refuges and temporary accommodation

'When they come to the refuge, everything else goes. Normality has all gone. Quite often, the only stability is within those school walls.'

A refuge children's worker

'Two-thirds of refuge residents are children. Inevitably they will have needs for protection and emotional and psychological support.'

Local Government Association 2006: 18

Schools and pre-schools can be islands of stability for children in temporary accommodation who have little routine or consistency in their lives. They can provide time out from family problems. The children and their parents will often have additional needs; it is helpful for education staff to understand the challenges and barriers to education faced by this group.

Families fleeing violence – children missing education

Concerns for the well-being of children are often a key part of a mother's decision to escape an abusive relationship and seek help. For some women, the process of leaving will take several months or even years and she may repeatedly return. Some mothers flee a succession of violent relationships. For children, this involves huge disruption and often several changes of school. If subsequently the abuser then returns to the family, this can cause emotional upheaval:

'She's taken six kids through the hostel and now he's back. I felt vicious. I didn't want to be near her or see her.'

A secondary school girl

'They've only been to two schools. I've made sure of that. It has meant them getting up at six to make sure they get the bus into town and out again. The kids get tired. We've been in 18 different houses.'

A mother

Children from families fleeing violence may miss out on weeks or even months of education. They face several barriers to attending school:

- families may be in time-limited temporary accommodation several miles from school
- mothers may put off finding new school places because of the temporary situation
- local schools may be full, or may not have places for all siblings
- travel costs to the previous school may be prohibitive
- mothers may be concerned about children being tracked down en route to and from school so may be reluctant to allow children to make the journey
- children may be reluctant to separate from their mother out of fear for her safety.

It can be helpful for children to be placed as soon as possible at a school close to their refuge or temporary accommodation.

Refuge children's workers have described considerable difficulties with secondary school admissions, with delays of weeks or even months between an application to the local authority and the start date. They have said the situation seems worse for children with behavioural needs, where requests for assessment and reports may increase the delay (however, this is contrary to government guidance, see Chapter 12). One child was reported to have returned to live with his father, simply so that he could continue with his education.

In the interim period, a child may be in a strange town with no social contacts and few financial means. At a refuge, young people may be privy to a lot of inappropriate information, simply because they are around when women are sharing their experiences of abuse with each other (Saunders and Humphreys 2002). In addition, having children off school and in cramped conditions can put an enormous strain on family relationships.

> 'Children should have access to e-learning or home tuition until a school placement can be found. Yet it never seems to happen.'
>
> A refuge children's worker

As well as the missed learning opportunities, a change of school brings about other problems: children may lose coursework; they may have to study different foreign languages or different syllabuses; options chosen in one school may not be available in the next. Children also lose their friends and their social networks; this can be particularly difficult for adolescents. It can also be frustrating for school staff, when they put much effort into settling a child, to see them move on after a few days or weeks – yet giving a child a positive school experience is never wasted work.

What is a refuge like for children and families?

The following information is provided for children on The Hideout (http://www.thehideout.org.uk), the web site for young people created by Women's Aid.

DO WE HAVE TO GO TO A REFUGE?

Women and children don't have to move to a refuge to get help. Most areas now have local support services that know about domestic violence and that can help women, children and young people through this. They can offer advice, information and support about staying safe and about the options available to you and your family.

Some areas also have local support for men who want to change their behaviour and want to stop being violent.

WHAT IS A REFUGE?

A refuge is a safe house where women and children can come to escape domestic violence at home. It's a safe place to stay temporarily, until things can be sorted out and your family either moves back to your old home or finds a new home.

At the refuge every family will have their own room, but there will be other women and children at the refuge you can talk to who've gone through a similar thing. There are also people working in the refuge (staff) who know about domestic violence and are there to support you, your brothers or sisters and your mum. Refuge staff can listen to your worries, talk to you about ways of staying safe and about what happens next. They'll help you and your family in whatever you choose to do.

HOW DO I FIND A REFUGE?

Refuges exist all over England, Scotland, Wales, Northern Ireland and the Republic of Ireland. Most refuges will take only women and their children. You or your mum can ring the Freephone 24 Hour National Domestic Violence Helpline on 0808 2000 247 (run in partnership between Women's Aid and Refuge) to get more information and to find a refuge. Some refuges will take in young women between the ages of 16–18 years on their own, without their mum.

The addresses of refuges are kept secret so that the women and children living there can be safe from their abusers.

WHAT'S A REFUGE LIKE FOR CHILDREN AND YOUNG PEOPLE?

Each refuge is different, but generally you would share a room with your mum and with your brothers and sisters. Usually about 4–8 families share a house in a refuge. In some refuges families share a sitting room, kitchen and bathroom, while in other refuges families may have their own bathroom and kitchen.

Most refuges have a playroom for children, and staff to support children and young people and plan activities for them. These Children's Support Workers are staff especially for children and young people and lots of kids find it helpful to talk to them about any worries they have or about what they've been through. Children and young people may go on outings, and often there are playschemes during the school holidays. Most refuges also have a garden with a play area for children.

DO I HAVE TO CHANGE SCHOOLS?

One of the most difficult things about moving to a refuge is having to leave your home and friends behind. Most children and young people will have to change schools as well, because either their old school is too far away from the refuge or it's not safe to go back to the old school.

The Children's Support Worker, or another staff member, will help you find a new school closer to the refuge. It's not easy changing schools in the middle of a term, but in a refuge there are lots of people who can help you with this change. You're not alone when you move to a refuge!

Reproduced with kind permission of Women's Aid Federation of England

The following is taken from the web site of the organisation Refuge (http://www.refuge.org.uk).

Any woman who has experienced domestic violence – emotional or physical – can go to a refuge, with or without children. Some refuges are specifically for women from particular ethnic or cultural backgrounds. Staff there understand the trauma women have experienced and can support women both practically and emotionally. There is also peer support – which can sometimes be the most beneficial support a woman can receive. Women stay in refuges for as long as they need. Some stay for a few days, others remain for months while they wait for accommodation in a new community. A refuge is temporary accommodation and women are helped to find more suitable permanent accommodation.

In practical terms refuge workers can assist in many areas:

- budgeting and welfare benefits
- accessing health services
- finding nurseries and schools
- accessing local community and cultural services
- gaining legal advice, including accompanying women to appointments and court
- safety planning
- training, education and employment
- finding permanent housing in a new community.

Refuges and minority ethnic families

'Out of an estimated 400 refuge support services in England, 40 are of a specialist nature, of which 28 are Asian refuges providing a total of 265 bed spaces (Thiara 2005 in NSPCC Inform 2008: 28). However, nine out of ten local authorities have no specialised black and minority ethnic service for abused women (Coy *et al.*) in NSPCC Inform 2008: 28.

The needs of children in refuges and temporary accommodation

'Imagine yourself waking up in a new place; you've not got your handbag or your phone, your purse, your hairbrush, your make-up, your address book, nothing. You're given someone else's clothes to put on, then you're packed off to start a new job. When you get there you've not got a seat; people look at you but no one speaks to you, you don't know what you're doing for your lunch, you don't know when you're finishing and you don't know why you're there either. How would you feel?

With acknowledgement to Oldham Family Crisis Group, who use the above as part of their training programme

Children may arrive at a refuge then have to go to a new school without the things that make them feel right: clothes that fit, hair gel and accessories, the right schoolbag, their lunchbox. These things will almost certainly not be a priority for a highly stressed mother who has fled her home in fear for her safety and that of her children. Yet particularly as children reach adolescence, looking right is crucial to feeling good.

Families often arrive at refuges with little more than what they are standing up in, having taken a sudden opportunity to flee violence. Starting a new school is daunting: these are some of our most vulnerable children; they will feel different and may have a different accent. They may be shocked and experiencing significant losses, though some children may have advanced coping skills and be good at putting on a brave face.

Young people and families may experience the following emotions and events.

- *Fear, anxiety and uncertainty.* Many children will have lived with huge stress and fear for their own safety and that of their mother. Research has found that 60 per cent of victims had left their partners because they were afraid they would be killed (Humphreys and Thiara 2002). Once in temporary accommodation, children continue to live with uncertainty about being tracked down and where they will go next. Some will have experienced prolonged physical and/or sexual abuse.
- *Anger, resentment, confusion and loss of control.* Children may have had no choice or say in what has happened. They may not have been consulted or fully understand why drastic changes have been forced on them. Some mothers will have worked to protect their children from knowing the extent of abuse. Children can be furious with their mother for making them leave their homes, schools and friends. They may love or have ambiguous feelings towards their father. Resentment can build up.

'One boy was banging his head and crying out, he was so angry with his mother, even though he would tell stories of his dad's abuse. His dad had been the carer and done lots with him – like going to the football. Mum was the breadwinner.'

A refuge children's worker

- *Loss and sudden hardship.* Some children will have had to leave all their possessions: their clothes, toys, mobile phone, computer and electronic games. They may have left their pets, friends, schools and, in some cases, siblings. There may be drastic financial implications to leaving, and cashflow problems.
- *New constraints.* Adjusting to refuge life can be stressful and put a strain on family relationships. The family may be in cramped accommodation in an unfamiliar town. Families may be sharing a room and have little privacy. Children may complain about over-crowding, other disruptive children, refuge rules, the restrictions on going out, restrictions on visitors (imposed because of the need to keep the location secret) and the tight security arrangements. Contact with grandparents or other extended family may be problematic. Teenagers may find little to do. For many, this will be a far cry from their previous accommodation.
- *Being ostracised by the community or other family members.* Children from ethnic minorities, whose mothers leave an abusive relationship, can be ostracised by their community and/or extended family. Being ostracised can happen in any community when people find it difficult to believe that someone they know and respect is an abuser; abusers will often say that their victims are mentally unstable, irrational or hysterical.
- *Relief and feelings of safety.* Many children have positive experiences of refuges and are relieved to feel safer. They can network with other young people who have suffered similar experiences (though turnover of new friends will be high and people may leave suddenly). Research found that children were generally positive about refuges, stating that they were happy to be away from the abuser and felt safer than they did in their own homes (Jarvis *et al.* 2005).

Other school issues

As well as the emotional turmoil that accompanies moving into temporary accommodation and starting a new school, young people may be embarrassed about their accommodation and therefore be vulnerable to teasing and bullying because there can be a stigma attached to living in a refuge.

'You have confidence if you live in a normal house and can afford to go to school … when I'm off … what'll they think? I don't want to lie, people have seen me around. People'll think she's nasty, she's from the hostel, they're all smackheads. I caught the bus and my friends were on it. Everyone was mithering me. Why have you been off for this long? I felt ashamed to come into school from the hostel, so I caught the next bus and I was on the buses all day.'

A secondary school girl

'She was angry and was a target for bullying about all the things going on in her life.'

A mother

MY SO CALLED LIFE?

MY SO CALLED LIFE WHERE HAS IT GONE?
I HAVE LOST MY SELF CONFIDENCE
AND MY FEELINGS AND PRIDE LOCKED UP INSIDE.
WHERE DO I TURN WHERE DO I GO?
I FEEL LIKE A BOMB, WAITING TO EXPLODE.
SO MANY PROBLEMS CAUSE SO MUCH STRIFE.
AT THE END OF THE DAY THAT'S MY SO CALLED LIFE.

By a boy aged 13

From the kids' page of Bolton Women's Aid Fortalice web site http://www.bwafortalice.org.uk/2.html
Reproduced with kind permission

Complex parenting issues

When a mother and her children leave her controlling, abusive partner, family dynamics change. Often, the male will have dictated the rules and the mother will have been subservient. The mother may then find it difficult to be assertive and impose boundaries. Once in the refuge, the children no longer know what they can and can't do, so they may test the new boundaries. They may not have confidence in their mother's parenting ability. They may model the perpetrator's behaviour and, in turn, be abusive to their mother.

'Violence and control may have been their norm and they are no longer exposed to it; this may be the first time they have had to reflect on or deal with it. This can bring a raft of issues to the fore.'

A family support worker

On arrival at a refuge, mothers may be at their most vulnerable: traumatised, depressed, exhausted, preoccupied with immediate practicalities, and emotionally unavailable for their children. They may feel guilty about their perceived parenting inadequacies, at what they are putting their children through, at not having done more to protect them.

'Suddenly mum had full parenting responsibilities and was really struggling. She seemed expressionless. … The mother needed some support with parenting; about the importance of praise and positive attention.'

A children's refuge worker

A children's refuge worker described the plight of some mothers from ethnic minorities who have lived with their extended family, where the mother-in-law has taken responsibility for parenting. When the mother moves to the refuge with the children to flee domestic violence, it is her first experience of parenting; the children have to get used to a new style and this adds to the stress on the family unit. Sometimes, and through no fault of her own, the mother may not know her baby's or child's routines. This experience is difficult for both the mother and her children.

Family support in refuges

Many refuges have designated children's workers. They help mothers and children to communicate and build a new sort of relationship; they help build a mother's confidence to parent and develop behaviour strategies. They organise activities that allow the family to have fun and enjoy time together, e.g. cooking and playing games. They advise mothers about explaining the situation to children and answering their questions. They advise on issues regarding contact with the abusing parent. The children's worker may assist with finding school places and settling the children.

'They made us do things as a family. Cooking. Altogether. It was about showing the kids I could do things with them.'

A mother

Summary

'Placement in temporary accommodation, often at a distance from previous support networks or involving frequent moves, can lead to individuals and families falling through the net and becoming disengaged from health, education, social care and welfare support systems.'

HM Government 2006: 209

Children in refuges and temporary accommodation are some of the most vulnerable in our schools. Many miss out on education; many have complex needs. In Part 2, we will consider how schools and pre-schools can support this group and their parents.

Chapter 5

The impact on mothers and on parenting

'There were days when I didn't exist; he saw through me and walked around me. I was invisible. There were days when I liked not existing. I closed down, stopped thinking, stopped looking. There were children out there but they had nothing to do with me. Their dirty faces swam in front of me. Their noises came from miles away.'

The Woman Who Walked Into Doors, Doyle 1996: 178

'Children grow up expecting their mothers to fulfil their needs, care for and protect them. They may not understand, in the context of domestic violence, why their mothers are unable to do this.'

Mullender *et al.* 2002: 157

At the heart of domestic violence lies the desire of one partner to have power and control over the other. Abusive and controlling behaviour deprives mothers of the authority, confidence, physical and emotional strength they need to parent effectively. We now consider in more detail the impact on mothers and consequently on their ability to parent.

The physical and psychological effects on mothers

Domestic violence is rarely a one-off incident and the impact on mothers can be profound. It causes lasting damage to physical and mental health and well-being. Physical injuries are common and include bruises and abrasions, fractured bones, lost teeth, internal injuries, gynaecological problems and miscarriages. However, for some women, the emotional and psychological abuse is just as serious and damaging as physical and sexual abuse, and can be longer lasting. Psychological abuse can result in self-harm and suicide. Many women carry the psychological scars long after the physical injuries have healed.

'He's always in my head, all the time.'

'I used to predict his every mood – I couldn't even open my mouth.'

Mothers interviewed by Warren Dodd (2004)

Domestic violence can precipitate a number of psychological and psychiatric problems including anxiety, depressive symptoms, and suicidal behaviour. It is a factor in at least one in four suicide attempts by women, and with repeated exposure to traumatic events, a proportion of individuals may develop Post-Traumatic Stress Disorder (PTSD). The impact of domestic violence has been found to have parallels with the torture and imprisonment of hostages (the Stockholm Syndrome). A significant percentage of women in touch with mental health services have had violent or abusive experiences. Women feel helpless, ashamed, lose confidence and may experience panic attacks.

A woman's ability to work, parent effectively and, after leaving a violent partner, to move on and build a new life, is affected:

'I was so depressed I was nearly sectioned.'

'I was so scared of getting lost in my own mind.'

'I was pillow hugging ... just sitting in the corner, screaming.'

'I was hospitalised. I didn't want to live – I hoped I wouldn't wake up.'

Mothers interviewed by Warren Dodd (2004)

Domestic violence in pregnancy

Over 30 per cent of domestic violence is known to start in pregnancy. Abuse frequently escalates at this time, possibly because of:

- jealousy of the unborn child
- feelings of exclusion
- attempts to end the pregnancy
- anxiety concerning the woman's contact with health professionals
- accusations of infidelity.

Being pregnant may serve to increase vulnerability rather than affording any protection from violence. One study found that 15 per cent of women were assaulted in the first four months of pregnancy and 17 per cent were physically abused during the last five months of pregnancy (Mezey 1997).

Some adverse outcomes of pregnancy and labour, such as miscarriage, low birth weight and stillbirth, may be attributable to traumatic domestic violence. The stress of abuse may lead to other consequences such as failure to obtain adequate nutrition, rest and medical care. Because of this the Department of Health promotes the use of a routine, universal, standardised screening system by doctors and midwives to encourage pregnant women to disclose domestic violence. Detecting domestic violence and taking appropriate action (such as giving advice about local helplines or refuge services) has the potential to break the cycle and to prevent a violent situation becoming one of repeated and intensifying victimisation.

Domestic violence, maternal depression and attachment

Many mothers living with domestic violence suffer depression. This adversely impacts upon parent–child relationships and attachment because those mothers are less likely to stimulate their babies and children. Murray and Cooper (1997) discuss the growing body of evidence indicating that post-natal depression is implicated in a range of adverse outcomes for babies, especially males, impacting on their cognitive and emotional development. Maternal depression can affect infant cognitive, behavioural and emotional functioning, effects that last beyond the mother's resumption of normal interaction with the infant (Weinberg and Tronick 1998).

Thus, babies are more likely to be deprived of quality parenting where domestic violence, with its associated levels of stress, is present. Although this does not imply that all women who have experienced domestic violence cause their children difficulties, the primary cause of disrupted parenting is the experience of violence and abuse.

The impact on the mother–baby relationship

Violence by a male partner has severe consequences on early mother–baby relationships.

- A partner's violence may create multiple and serious stressors for a mother, which interfere with her ability to respond sensitively to her baby. There is much research showing the importance of responsive and sensitive mothering in the healthy development of children.
- Violence in the home can cause a mother to become depressed, distracted and emotionally drained, thus reducing her ability to be emotionally available and attentive and sensitive to her children's needs (Holden and Ritchie 1991).
- A mother may set enormously high standards for herself and her baby by trying to have a 'non-crying' baby so that her violent partner will not be 'provoked' by a noisy or demanding baby.

The impact on parenting

Domestic violence affects parenting in a number of ways and can severely undermine the relationships that a mother has with her children (Mullender et al. 2002). If a mother is depressed, stressed and preoccupied with the need to keep the peace and appease a partner, she may lack the emotional and physical resources that parenting demands. Women can be so worn down both physically and emotionally that they disengage from the family. This is a terrible feeling and gives rise to much guilt and self-blame. In terms of Maslow's Hierarchy of Needs (Maslow 1970), if a woman does not feel safe and secure in her home, if she is always concerned for the safety of herself and her children, then she is unlikely to be able to move up to the next levels of 'love and belonging' and 'esteem'.

What staff in schools or pre-schools may see is a mother who appears passive, disengaged or uncaring. Schools have raised concerns about mothers who seem disorganised, can't get the children to school on time, send the children in looking unkempt or dirty, leave the children to sort themselves out in the mornings, rely on siblings to care for each other, shout a lot or seem emotionally distant. Concerns can rightly be raised about parental neglect – while behind the scenes can be a desperate, depressed or even injured mother in need of help.

The reality could be that the regular contact with staff or parents at pre-school or school is the main social contact for the mother outside the immediate family.

Domestic violence may cause rifts in the relationship between a mother and her children. In many families, it is omnipresent and affects everyone, yet very few children and

abused parents talk to each other about the fear and violence that is happening or has happened at home.

> 'Despite its visible effects, domestic violence is often like "the elephant in the corner" – very obvious to all family members but never mentioned. Inevitably, this silence damages the relationship between mother and child, increasing their isolation and helplessness.'
>
> Saunders and Humphreys 2002: 97

Some examples of adverse effects that domestic violence has on parenting are as follows.

- A mother may have difficulties performing everyday childcare tasks such as getting the children up and out, providing breakfast, the right equipment and helping them organise themselves for the day.
- A mother who is undermined by a controlling partner or partners (and this can often be over a period of years) may find it difficult to discipline her children and impose behaviour boundaries herself, even after the family are away from the abuser. Guilt feelings and over-compensation may continue because the mother feels she did not stand up for herself or protect her children.
- Children may perceive their mother as weak and unable to protect them from harm. They can feel angry with their mother for this.
- Children may be led by a violent partner to understand that their mother is bad, so is getting punished; an impression that is reinforced by the accompanying verbal abuse (Mullender *et al.* 2002). Children may learn to excuse their father and blame their mother.

- The parent–child role can become reversed; the child, especially an older child, can be the one person the mother can turn to for support and understanding. Yet this can provoke further criticism and aggression from the father.
- A mother can be isolated by the violent partner from support networks – from other parents and from extended family. In the playground, a mother may seem isolated, not socialising with other parents or carers.
- Children can be forced to take part in abuse of the mother – leading to feelings of terrible guilt and confusion.

Why don't women 'just leave'?

Mothers are often held accountable for failure to deal with violent men (Edleson 1999), yet there can be huge obstacles to women leaving a violent relationship. Examples of the many practical, social and emotional factors that can make leaving difficult include:

- fear of further violence
- lack of knowledge about how and where to access help
- nowhere to go
- economic dependence
- wanting to keep the family united for the sake of the children
- not wanting to uproot the children
- social isolation
- emotional dependence
- lack of confidence
- cultural, religious or immigration issues (see below).

Because of these factors, it may take some time and several temporary separations before women are able permanently to escape the abusive relationship.

Particular issues for mothers from black and ethnic minority communities and their children

- The pressures on Asian women to keep domestic violence a secret may be stronger than in some other cultures. Asian women represent their family when they marry; consequently if a marriage fails they may be seen as to blame and to be affecting the family's honour (Shah-Kazemi 2001; Rai and Thiara 1997, in Home Office 2005b).
- Religious beliefs may impinge on the mother's willingness to leave a violent marriage; for example, in a marriage following Islamic principles, the woman enters into a contract with her husband, which only he can terminate. He can prevent a religious divorce from his wife if he wishes to, even if she has obtained a legal divorce. This leaves the woman with additional stress. She may feel trapped between her religious beliefs and the culture in which the family are living (Home Office 2005b).
- Immigration status can also affect the desire to seek help; for example, if the mother has come to this country for marriage, there is not only increased pressure for it to be successful, but also the problem of being in an unfamiliar country, with a foreign language to contend with and no knowledge of life outside the home, such as public

transport, services available for support and so on (Home Office 2005b). She may be threatened by the family with deportation and her passport may be taken from her.

Summary

Domestic violence severely undermines parenting. One of the most important things education settings can do to support children is to support the abused parent. In Chapter 8, we describe some strategies.

Chapter 6

Summary

Domestic violence and the 'Every Child Matters' Five Key Outcomes

In Part 1, we have explored how domestic violence affects every aspect of a child's education and well-being. It is identified by the government as a cause of vulnerability in children, which has a negative impact on their ability to achieve their full potential across the 'Every Child Matters' Five Key Outcomes. The Government aims for every child, whatever their background or their circumstances, to have the support they need to:

Be healthy (i.e. physically, mentally, sexually and emotionally healthy; have a healthy lifestyle; choose not to take illegal drugs).

In families where there is domestic violence, children are often abused by the violent parent and suffer the trauma of hearing or witnessing the abuse of the non-violent parent; the impact on mental health can be long-term. Children's health can suffer if domestic violence reduces the parenting ability of the non-abusing parent. It can impair the parent–child relationship. Domestic violence can lead to extreme risk-taking behaviour and self-harm.

Stay safe (i.e. safe from neglect, violence, abuse, sexual exploitation, bullying and discrimination, accidental injury or death, crime and anti-social behaviour, have security, stability and be cared for).

Nearly three-quarters of children on the 'at-risk' register live in households where domestic violence occurs (Department of Health 2002). Men who are violent to their female partners are also likely to be violent to their children. Children do not feel safe – and often are not safe – in their home. Children's emotional and behavioural difficulties can lead to truancy and periods of exclusion, placing children at greater risk of anti-social behaviour, crime, abuse and sexual exploitation. Domestic violence is also linked to higher incidence of miscarriage, low birth weight, prematurity, foetal injury and foetal death (McWilliams and McKiernan 1993).

Enjoy and achieve (i.e. school attendance, enjoyment and achievement, personal and social development).

Children experiencing domestic violence face considerable barriers to school attendance, participation and enjoyment. Education may be disrupted by repeated changes of home and school and/or children may opt to stay at home to be near their mothers. Concentration and readiness for learning is affected; the stress and anxiety means children may not pursue their interests, relax and enjoy school. Domestic violence can lead to social isolation. Pre-schoolers are particularly affected (Hughes 1988; Rossman et al. 1994); they are thought to witness more violence than school-aged children, yet have fewer emotional and cognitive resources to withstand the impact. Additional caring responsibilities can be placed on older children.

Make a positive contribution (i.e. engage in decision making and support the community and environment, engage in law-abiding and positive behaviour, develop positive relationships and develop self-confidence, successfully deal with significant life changes and challenges, develop enterprising behaviour).

Domestic violence impacts on children's confidence and makes it difficult for them to engage fully in the community and form healthy relationships. It affects how children relate to each other. Children often feel they are to blame for violence in their family; this can diminish their self-esteem and can make it difficult for them to develop positive relationships. Many children affected by domestic violence have emotional and behavioural difficulties. They have higher rates of depression, anxiety and trauma symptoms (McCloskey *et al.* 1995).

Achieve economic well-being (i.e. access to further education, readiness for employment, access to transport, access to material goods, live in a decent home in a household free from low income).

Domestic violence places children at risk of financial hardship. An abused parent can face difficulties working and in maintaining a job. Children are likely to suffer financial hardship if they flee the family home with their mother. Children who have had a disrupted education are less likely to achieve their academic potential.

With acknowledgement to the Local Government Association 2006

Part 2

Meeting children's needs in schools and early years settings

Chapter 7

Introduction

'Domestic violence is likely to have a damaging effect on the health and development of children, and it is often appropriate for such children to be regarded as children in need. ... Everyone working with women and children should be alert to the frequent inter-relationship between domestic violence and the abuse and neglect of children.'

HM Government 2006: 202

Every school and early years setting is likely to have children who are affected by domestic violence. The professionals within are often the first people outside the family to pick up on the distress of a child or parent and make the link to family issues.

Staff may feel there is little that can be done in the face of problems that stem from home, or that other – more specialist services – are better placed to address those problems. Yet most families who experience domestic violence do not have involvement from specialist services. Working positively with the non-abusing parent is an important way of protecting and supporting the child. Schools and pre-schools may be the only provider of support outside friends and extended family.

In Part 2, we consider the ways in which schools and pre-schools can support young people and their families. We look at:

- ways education settings can support the non-abusing parent
- the needs of young children in early years settings
- how schools can support children affected by domestic violence; how they can respond to children's pastoral and behaviour needs
- how children can be helped to talk and to understand
- the roles of different professionals and ways schools and pre-schools can work with them
- key government guidance
- some safety and confidentiality issues that settings may encounter
- preventative work; how organisations can educate young people and the community
- education and training resources.

The Committee on Home Affairs recommended the following (House of Commons, Home Affairs Committee 2008):

- training for all education professionals on domestic violence, forced marriage and 'honour'-based violence
- ensuring there is a designated member of staff with responsibility for domestic violence and forced marriage issues, whose responsibilities include whole school training
- all Postgraduate Certificate in Education and professional development training to include modules on violence against women
- OfSTED being tasked to inspect schools on their success or failure in tackling domestic violence and forced marriage.

Staff need to be informed about domestic violence; about appropriate actions to take and support services that are available. As long as a child is in school or pre-school and can access adults with an understanding of domestic violence issues, there will always be ways to offer support.

Chapter 8

Engaging and supporting parents

'Often, supporting the non-violent parent is likely to be the most effective way of promoting the child's welfare.'

Department for Education and Skills 2006: 203

'There are signs that something is really wrong in the family, the little girl seems anxious and unkempt, her father appears highly controlling and her mother is rarely seen. Yet there is no tangible evidence of abuse and I don't seem to be able to engage the mother. What should I do?'

A deputy head teacher

In Part 1 we described the detrimental effect of domestic violence on parenting; in particular, how it can deprive mothers of the authority, confidence, physical and emotional strength to parent effectively. Domestic violence damages the parent–child relationship. It can make it difficult for a mother to be emotionally available, play and interact positively with her children, and impose behaviour boundaries.

Education professionals can support children by supporting their mothers. However, fear of an abuser can make it very difficult for a mother to be open with staff and express concerns or feelings. Staff should not interpret an apparent reluctance to engage as not caring; a challenge is to build a trusting relationship and facilitate opportunities to talk.

Professionals who can reach out to the abused parent have often been key in improving the life chances of children. Many mothers who have left abusive relationships emphasised that they initially accessed help through school. Often one member of staff made the crucial difference: picked up that something was wrong, raised the issue and helped the mother understand the negative impact of the abuse on her children. It is through education settings that a mother may access help, make changes, begin to re-build her life and repair relationships with her children.

'School were the only people who supported us. They called a child in need meeting and they knew what was available. They were aware of what my kids had been through.'

A mother

Pre-schools and schools can provide information about sources of support to mothers by displaying it in waiting areas with notice boards or leaflet racks. Posters and leaflets displayed prominently also give the message that the institution is aware of, and takes a stand on, the issue.

> 'After it had all come out, I got a leaflet from school about domestic abuse and there were quotes from children that described just the sort of thing my child had been through. If only we'd had that before.'
>
> A mother

Engaging parents and building trust

Pre-schools and primary schools are ideally placed to reach out to mothers in need of help. Mothers visit regularly, often without their abusive partner. Drop-off and pick-up times may be a mother's best or only opportunity for a chat with someone outside the family who has picked up that something is amiss. A mother may need help but may feel so low and powerless that she does not seek it – so the onus may be on staff to reach out to her.

Developing a relationship can take time, commitment and sensitivity; trust is paramount. A relationship does not happen overnight and we have described why mothers may feel they need to keep authorities at a distance. Mothers want someone who can understand their circumstances but not judge them.

> 'You've got to build on that relationship with mum. Start trying to get her thinking. Accepting that she needs support from different agencies. You're going to be chipping away at that for months.'
>
> A family support worker

> 'Quite often we are the first people mothers have spoken to. I know a family where the violence has been going on for years. The children are 13 or 14 and no one's talked. Often it's a case of sitting there and listening. The mothers need to talk to someone, they need to recognise it's not their fault. We'll continue to offer support and we may refer on to other agencies; adult mental health, for example.'
>
> A family support worker

Some tips for school staff on engaging and building trust include:

- try to see the woman separately from her partner
- be open; provide a listening ear
- give her a private space and time to talk – it may help to ask open-ended, non-threatening questions, for example, 'How are things at home?'

> 'A lady arrived at the refuge last week and I phoned the head teacher of her son's school to say they were safe. The head had had an inkling there were family problems; there was absenteeism, poor punctuality, a lack of uniform. She had no idea that this was due to the domestic violence, the mother being unable to get out of the house, being barricaded in. Things like that were preventing the boy from coming to school.
>
> Since then, mum has spent an afternoon talking to the head teacher about all her

experiences; now there's a completely different understanding. The head teacher said she wished the mother had told her this before; she could have done so much more to help; but obviously the mum didn't know how to. I mean, how do you knock on the head teacher's door? It's daunting. A lot of ladies don't have the best experiences of school themselves. If people felt more able to talk, I'm sure they would.'

A children's refuge worker

Mothers disclosing domestic violence

Guidance to staff when a mother discloses domestic violence to them includes:

- try to find somewhere quiet to talk
- keep calm and listen to what she has to say; remember that she may have chosen you because you are a good listener
- she may feel that it is her fault – tell her that domestic violence is common but is unacceptable and she is not to blame
- talk about confidentiality – if children are living with domestic violence, whether or not they are directly involved, it is a child protection issue and the procedures in place in your school or pre-school should be explained
- it is inappropriate to try and encourage her to leave the situation – this is her decision
- find out if she or the children are in any immediate danger and let her know that she can make phone calls from school if she needs to
- offer ongoing support and give her information about helplines and local sources of support if she wants them
- arrange to meet with her again if that would help her.

Keep informed about your setting's child protection procedures so you are confident about how to handle disclosures.

'The main thing was that I had complete trust in the school. I knew that if I told the headmaster, he wouldn't do anything behind my back without telling me.'

A mother

Staff may feel concerned about how a mother might react to them contacting social care, or seeking her permission to call a multi-agency Common Assessment Framework meeting, yet many parents have spoken positively about the outcome. One mother described the blanket of support she subsequently received from different authorities:

'What made the difference was school, social services, the domestic violence counsellor ... everyone worked together. They made me realise what I'd done, what I'd put the kids through. They encouraged me to tell my mother about my drugs habit. Once she knew, it was completely the opposite of what I'd expected. It was the fear of losing my kids that made me change. It had to go that far.'

Professionals should be aware of the many practical, social and emotional reasons why women don't 'just leave' and why leaving is extremely difficult (see Chapter 5).

Some barriers to parents engaging with schools and pre-schools

'It is vital that professionals are aware of the power and control dynamics of domestic violence, recognise this as a child protection issue and do not allow perpetrators to manipulate the situation. This means talking to the parents separately and recognising when the presence of an abuser makes it impossible for children, or the non-abusing parent, to express their wishes or feelings.'

Local Government Association 2006: 14

Parents generally want the best for their children, yet some will have reasons to be wary of authorities and may seem to want to keep a distance.

*   The mother may be aware of the 'can of worms' she will open by disclosing information. She may fear for her safety and that of her children.
*   Often the mother is depressed and carrying the burden of guilt about the impact of abuse on the children. Being open can be difficult.
*   Many mothers say their greatest fear is that their children will be taken into care. Abusive partners know this and often intimidate their victims by threatening to contact social services (Local Government Association 2006: 15).
*   The mother may feel troublesome and unwelcome because her children cause the school problems, e.g. because of poor attendance, punctuality and behaviour, and uniform issues.
*   The mother may feel threatened by 'authority' figures.
*   The mother may fear the abuser trying to obtain residency of the child by arguing that allegations are malicious and that the mother is mentally unstable.

Contrary to some stereotypical perceptions of a mother who is a victim of domestic violence being weak, many abused mothers are strong characters, trying to do the best for their children in very challenging circumstances. Sometimes staff interpret a mother's reluctance to engage with school, or her child's lack of compliance with rules on homework and uniform, as evidence that she is unsupportive, uncaring or incompetent. A pre-school or school can unwittingly add to the mother's bad feelings about herself and it is easy to see how institutions can raise rather than lower barriers to communication. For example:

*   A parent said that she would sometimes leave her daughter's primary school in tears after feeling she had been 'told off' at a meeting for all the things that she was not doing: reading, the right uniform, homework.
*   A parent received several calls a week from different teachers at her son's secondary school, saying that he was in trouble, though some were to say he had had a great lesson. She dreaded the next bad news phone call. This added to her stress. Things improved when the school designated one member of staff for all home–school communication.

Positive partnerships are important. Where there are complex issues and a number of professionals involved, education settings should consider appointing one key worker for home–school communication.

Supporting children and families from ethnic minorities

Women from ethnic minority groups, and especially those who have a limited knowledge of English, may find it particularly difficult to access help for themselves and their children. There can be communication barriers, a lack of familiarity with the education system, health and social care services, and poor accessibility of services. Education professionals may be anxious about being seen to be interfering in a different culture's practices and beliefs. In fact, staff may be able to provide a key link to support services; staff have an important role.

The family support worker role

'The support worker in school has been absolutely fabulous. She gives me advice, reports on what has happened in school. She knows our family.'

A mother

'They know me, see me out and about, walking round the estates; we mingle, make ourselves known; walk about, we build a relationship that way. We will be out on the drive at home time; some parents may get out of the car and come and talk.'

A family support worker

Many schools and children's centres now have family support worker posts or employ learning mentors. Their brief includes work in the community and home visits. They can provide a vital link between school and home. Through working closely with parents, family support workers can often 'find the missing piece of the jigsaw' and help schools make sense of a child's behaviour or attendance difficulties.

These workers will frequently encounter domestic violence issues, so it is important they receive appropriate training and supervision. They should be clear about the roles of other supporting agencies and how to refer on. They may be able to access places on holiday schemes or at youth clubs; they may know of additional support for families and children provided by social care or the voluntary sector.

A space to talk

'My ideal setting for working with families would be an informal room, like a front room, with settees, maybe a TV in there; where they could just come and sit and talk, cry, laugh, whatever they wanted. Just away from everything else. That would be fantastic. I think every school needs this. Right now, I use this office, the library, an interview room ... wherever.'

A family support worker

Increasingly, children's centres and schools are planned with community facilities in mind. A designated family space for meetings and parent groups is invaluable.

Home visits

There are many reasons why a mother may be wary of coming into school; it is important to find ways of reaching out to her. A home visit can be a good option: being less intimidating for a parent who feels negative about school, or has been called in when her child is in trouble. Home can be a more relaxed place for an open and uninterrupted conversation. However, be aware that if there is domestic violence, the mother may worry her partner will return home during a visit. Schools have reported cases where a violent partner has been at home and listening from upstairs. Professionals should assess personal risk around conducting home visits and follow their school or local authority guidelines.

This is the approach taken by one family support worker:

> 'Where domestic violence is known about or suspected, I will do a home visit. We'll see mum and get a history. I ask the question routinely and outright. You need to be as open and honest as you possibly can be. You can't go round the houses with a question like that. It's not always about hitting. It can be more psychological. We'll discuss what it is and if she or the children have experienced it.
>
> I don't think we've had anyone resenting being asked. Mostly, they're happy to discuss it. Often, they don't always associate their child's difficult behaviour with domestic violence, with what the child has witnessed. People can be blinkered. So it makes parents think ... or see it from a completely different angle.'

Others workers may feel less comfortable about being so direct, but may provide openings to help a parent talk, allowing her to have more control in the interaction; allowing her to decide whether to trust this visitor. One family support worker said she left appointment cards with helplines printed on the back – a discreet way of passing on information.

Summary

Working in partnership with the non-abusing parent or carer is an important way of protecting and supporting children in domestic violence situations. It can make a real difference to families. Mothers particularly appreciate staff who cared for them, treating them as partners in planning, rather than pitying them or seeing them as weak.

One document recommends 'routine questioning and the provision of information about domestic violence by all service providers in regular contact with children and young people' (Local Government Association 2006: 22). This happens in health services. Women identified during ante-natal or post-natal checks have been referred to Sure Start Local Programmes and offered advice about agencies to contact (Niven and Ball 2007). However, staff may need training before feeling confident about routine questioning.

There is much that education settings can do to support parents. Some key points are as follows.

• Developing a relationship based on trust is key, but this takes time and perseverance.

There is no guarantee a woman will disclose, or want to be helped to move out of her situation.

- When a parent discloses domestic violence, child protection procedures have to be followed. Failing to share information or doing so inappropriately can put the victim and children at risk.
- Family support workers can provide emotional and practical support that can help the parent to re-engage with her children more confidently.
- Having a comfortable, relaxing family room is ideal, but if unavailable staff may have to be inventive in finding a quiet space.
- Supportive staff in education settings can help a parent develop or re-gain confidence. However, negative or critical comments about parenting skills can seriously undermine parenting skills and further disable the parent.
- Many parents have spoken positively of the support they received from professionals in the education, social care, health and voluntary sectors. Professionals can provide a package of care to support the parent and children.

'It was thanks to the domestic violence workers that I was able to keep my life together. C. held the kids together and M. held me together. I'm a new woman, I can go forward. We didn't fall apart and the kids are doing well.'

A mother

Chapter 9

Meeting children's needs in early years settings

'For too long, children under five who experience domestic violence have gone unheard and unrecognised. These children need accessible support services, provided by people who are trained in and aware of the significant impact of domestic violence.'

Refuge 2005: 4

'Research shows that positive early experiences enhance the likelihood of a better long-term outcome and increase [children's] likelihood of developing resilience in adversity, so that later stressful events are less likely to be traumatic.'

Murray and Andrews 2000: 167

In Chapter 2, the adverse effects of domestic violence on babies and young children were described and indicators of infant stress and trauma listed. Growing up with domestic violence can impact on an infant's social, emotional, behavioural, speech and language and cognitive development.

More children are accessing early years education through initiatives such as Sure Start in children's centres. Early years settings can make a considerable difference to the lives of young children who have experienced domestic violence and those of their parents or carers. Staff need training so they can recognise the signs, be aware of appropriate agencies for referrals and understand about safeguarding children.

Key to improving the life chances of pre-school children is to support their mothers. We now consider:

- ways pre-schools can support mothers and help them engage with different services
- intervention programmes that can support mothers and strengthen their relationships with their young children
- ways pre-school settings can meet some of the social, emotional, behavioural and other pastoral needs of young children who live with domestic violence.

Pre-school settings supporting mothers

Professionals in children's centres and other pre-school settings can support parents in a variety of ways. These include the following:

- providing information about community resources and sources of help (see Chapter 14). The parent, neighbours, family or concerned friends might respond to poster campaigns, leaflets or other information they pick up at pre-school;
- working closely with professionals from different agencies. These could be health visitors, social care staff, refuge staff, psychology services, pre-school special needs services, Women's Aid, police domestic violence co-ordinators, local counselling services;

'Sure Start children's centres are in an excellent position to contribute to the development of multi-agency teams and work on local strategies.'

Niven and Ball 2007: 8

- supporting access to positive parenting courses (e.g. Webster-Stratton);
- providing or supporting access to specialist parenting programmes and groups for women experiencing domestic abuse. Research suggests that child behaviour management interventions are less effective when parents are distressed (Webster-Stratton and Hammond 1990: 319–37), so parent groups run specifically for victims of domestic violence can also respond to the wider needs of this group;
- helping parents and young children build better relationships through play;
- helping parents keep medical appointments. Some children do not have their hearing, visual or other health needs diagnosed because of failure to attend. With parent consent, settings can request notification of appointments, so they can support the mother to keep them.

The previous chapter highlighted the importance of building a relationship of trust with the mother. Training provided for staff on Sure Start Local Programmes emphasises the importance of listening to the woman, though never harassing her into disclosing or leaving her partner; training also includes information on who to pass child protection information on to and sources of local advice and support (Niven and Ball 2007).

Below are details of an example of a successful pre-school multi-agency initiative; a group at a children's centre, for mothers and young children who had experienced domestic violence (Warren Dodd 2004). It was staffed by professionals from a variety of agencies: a specialist health visitor, an educational psychologist, children's centre staff, a Women's Aid child support worker and a social worker. It aimed to provide support for mothers and support positive interactions with their children. The project had three aspects to it:

- a specialist parenting/support group for the mothers
- therapeutic play experiences for children
- positive play sessions with mothers and young children together to build better relationships.

'Parenting can be a lonely responsibility, especially when compounded by an anxious awareness that all is not well with a child or in the family. Probably the single most therapeutic element in a group is the discovery that one is not alone in one's plight.'

Behr 1997: 121

Study of successful specialist parenting/support groups for mothers

The aims of the children's centre support group mentioned above were to:

- promote positive, sensitive parenting. There is a strong focus on enhancing the mother–child relationship
- provide women with the opportunity to discuss their own life concerns (e.g. housing, health issues, personal stress and worries)
- facilitate relationships with other mothers and provide social networks
- improve confidence and self-esteem
- help mothers understand and start resolving their own issues
- help mothers understand the experiences of their children.

Group interventions for parents can be a cost-effective and acceptable alternative to individual therapy, and groups may be particularly suitable for enhancing parenting behaviour. The best results come from interventions that highlight enjoyment and mutual pleasure and focus on parental empowerment and involvement.

Feedback from mothers in the group focused on the welcome opportunity to meet and talk with others in similar circumstances:

'The group was just what I needed before I moved out of the refuge.'

'When you are in domestic violence you think there is only you.'

'It made you realise you are not stupid or going off your head.'

'It's needed but it's painful.'

Therapeutic play experiences for children

The baby or young child takes the lead and makes choices in therapeutic play; it is a process that fosters cognitive and social development and communication skills. Play can be a form of therapy and can help young children to project their feelings. Children, particularly younger ones, may communicate through role play, puppets, small world (miniature) toys, drawing and painting.

Positive outcomes in this initiative were:

- the mothers became more positive in their comments about their own children
- they were more aware of the impact of domestic violence on the children
- they found out that people in a variety of agencies could help.

Mothers and group leaders thought the children had enjoyed and benefited from the group. Several commented on improvements in the children's behaviour:

'K is eating and talking better – I'm happier and less stressed.'

'Some of the children were quite aggressive and had very few boundaries – they calmed down a lot as the group went on.'

'One or two were very timid but they developed in confidence.'

Positive play sessions with mothers and young children

'The interactive process most protective against later violence begins in the first year after birth; the formation of a secure attachment relationship with a primary caregiver.'

Karr-Morse and Wiley 1997: 52

For some parents, the joys of parenting young children are overshadowed by a distressing family life. A mother may simply be too depressed, preoccupied or lack the emotional strength to play or even communicate much with her young child. She may have had her parenting skills undermined.

Pre-school staff and family support workers helped re-build relationships and re-establish the 'emotional availability' of mothers. They facilitated their having time and space with their children and modelled the enjoyment of shared activities, for example, playing, cooking and painting. They highlighted and praised the child's skills, achievements and progress. The emphasis was on mutual enjoyment. Each session ended with lunch and party/activity bags – to continue activities at home.

'They made us do things as a family. Cooking for example. All together – it was about showing the kids I could do things with them.'

A mother in a refuge

Aspects of Theraplay (Jernberg and Booth 1999) were incorporated into these sessions. The aim was to build more positive relationships between mothers and their children and encourage parental sensitivity.

The activities emphasised eye contact, touch, physical closeness, rhythmic movements and mutual enjoyment. Theraplay activities for mothers and children included:

- joint play (e.g. bubbles)
- art and craft activities (e.g. card making)
- games (e.g. pass the parcel)
- singing/action rhymes involving body contact (e.g. Row, Row, Row the Boat; Round and Round the Garden, Rock-a-Bye Baby).

How early years settings can meet young children's personal, social and emotional needs

The Early Years Foundation Stage (Department for Children, Schools and Families 2008c) describes how early years practitioners can support the development, learning and care of young children. The principles guiding the work of early years practitioners are grouped into four themes.

A *Unique Child* – every child is a competent learner from birth who can be resilient, capable, confident and self-assured.

Positive Relationships – children learn to be strong and independent from a base of loving and secure relationships with parents and/or a key person.

Enabling Environments – the environment plays a key role in supporting and extending children's development and learning.

Learning and Development – children develop and learn in different ways and at different rates, and all areas of learning and development are equally important and inter-connected.

Within the Early Years Foundation Stage there are six areas of Learning and Development. The first area is Personal, Social and Emotional Development, and within this area the following early learning goals are vital for all children but may be particularly relevant to those who have experienced domestic violence:

- be confident to try new activities
- respond to significant experiences, showing a range of feelings where appropriate
- have a developing awareness of their own needs, views and feelings, and be sensitive to the needs, views and feelings of others
- form good relationships with adults and peers
- understand what is right, what is wrong and why
- consider the consequences of their words and actions for themselves and others
- understand that people have different needs, views, cultures and beliefs that need to be treated with respect.

Infants from backgrounds of domestic violence may display troubling behaviours that relate to their experiences (see Chapter 2). Staff in pre-schools may observe children who:

- find separation from their main caregiver extremely distressing
- are reluctant to attend the setting
- are overly clingy to adults
- lack confidence
- appear hyperactive and inclined to aggression directed at adults and their peers
- respond negatively to direction from adults
- appear passive, quiet, avoidant of others and reluctant to engage with certain play or social activities
- have not learned about sharing and turn-taking
- fear new people or situations
- show high levels of distress, irritability or anxiety
- have delayed language and/or cognitive development
- are delayed with toileting/have frequent accidents
- are tired because of sleep disturbance and nightmares.

Of course, the above may also be indicators of other problems or developmental difficulties.

It is not always possible to provide an ideal home environment; however, boosting a child's resilience enhances the likelihood of a better long-term outcome.

'Early childhood education may be viewed as an innovative mental health strategy that affects many risk and protective factors.'

Weissberg 2000

People who educate and care for a child who has experienced domestic violence worry about how it will affect the child. Children, regardless of their age, do respond to what is going on around them. However, the impact and the recovery depend on many things. Early years settings can do a lot to help.

Excellent practice in early years settings benefits all children. Those from backgrounds where domestic violence is a factor may be more vulnerable and will particularly benefit from the following aspects of high quality early years care and education:

- good physical care – some young children may arrive tired, hungry and thirsty
- an understanding of attachment and its relevance to children who need warm, caring relationships with a small number of people
- predictability, routine and a secure base
- quality sensory experiences; opportunities for peace, quiet and relaxation
- a sensitive response to separation anxiety
- an appropriate and sensitive response to distress
- opportunities for both free and adult-structured play with other children
- adults who are aware of when to intervene with a child's play and when to stand back
- a language-rich environment with opportunities and encouragement to talk and be listened to
- encouragement for children to recognise and express feelings
- adults who can nurture the child and communicate that he or she is unique and valued.

The importance of quality play experiences

For all children, play is of vital importance. It is a fun, normal and very important part of growing up. Play helps children learn and practise communication, be creative and develop problem-solving and physical skills. Children who have experienced domestic violence usually have confused feelings that are hard to talk about. They often have low self-esteem and self-confidence, which may be shown by not wanting to try new things. Play is one of the easiest and safest ways for children to express how they are feeling. Play can help them develop their confidence and work through their worries. It can help adults strengthen their relationship with their children and understand how they see their world.

Young children need lots of affection, care and reassurance (hugs, playing, positive words). It is important they learn from an early age about acceptable behaviour, for example, it's never alright to hit or hurt anyone. Adults can show troubled children warmth and empathy and respond sensitively to their distress.

Summary

All early years practitioners should be aware that domestic violence may underlie worrying behaviour in young children. Quality experiences in the early years settings can support social, emotional and cognitive development, build confidence and develop communication skills. Early years settings are well placed to offer support to mothers.

Chapter 10

Supporting school-aged children

Introduction

'It really did help to tell someone so I could get it off my chest, instead of holding it in all the time. I can go, whenever, to my learning mentor ... if someone is pushing you, it eases stuff.'

A secondary school girl

'Experience and consultation with children, shows that they will talk about their concerns and problems to people who they feel they can trust and feel confident with. This will not necessarily be a teacher. It is therefore essential that all staff and volunteers in a school, FE college or other education establishment know how to respond sensitively to a child's concerns, who to approach for advice about them, and the importance of not guaranteeing complete confidentiality.'

Department for Education and Skills 2006: 72

Many young people affected by domestic violence have significant emotional, pastoral, behavioural and learning needs. Some may have wide-ranging social and emotional difficulties, be angry or disruptive. Others may dissociate, be withdrawn and internalise their feelings. Anxiety about home events may distract from learning. Attendance and punctuality may be poor, or children may have missed out on periods of education.

Education professionals can notice distress and monitor well-being. They can listen and help a child with their thinking and understanding; they can give vulnerable children a boost, provide additional pastoral care and behaviour support; they can refer on to other supporting agencies. Education settings can make a real difference.

In this chapter we will consider how schools can meet some of these children's needs. We describe:

- the role of the key adult
- some techniques for helping children to express their feelings and anxieties
- safety planning with children
- appropriate responses to disclosures of domestic violence
- ways of meeting the pastoral needs
- ways of meeting behaviour needs.

Of course, not all children from abusive backgrounds will have problems with learning and behaviour in school. For some, losing themselves in school and schoolwork will provide relief and an escape. Yet it is important to recognise that some children who show few external symptoms and behave well may, nonetheless, be anxious, unhappy and have significant emotional needs.

The key adult role

'If this is happening in your family, remember that you are not alone. Domestic abuse happens in many families and there are people that can help you and your family. Everyone has the right to be and feel safe'.
http://www.thehideout.org.uk/under10/whatisdomesticabuse/default.aspa
Reproduced with the kind permission of Women's Aid Federation of England

Two key issues emerged from research among eight- to sixteen-year-olds into what helped them cope and what support they needed (Mullender *et al.* 2002). These were:

• being listened to and taken seriously as participants in the domestic violence situation; and
• being actively involved in finding solutions and in helping to make decisions.

Trusting relationships with supportive adults in school can be of prime importance to young people. Parents and children have spoken passionately about the difference one key person made; usually someone who understood the background, could empathise, monitor and provide a listening ear. This person may also have provided behaviour support. For many, this was crucial to maintaining their school place.

'I see Mr P. every day, morning and afternoon. He's my best teacher. You need someone to see every day. ... Yesterday I was in deep trouble. Wound up. I started swearing, calling. One of the learning support people came to the rescue.'

A secondary school boy

'There are staff who understand his temperament ... If there is agitation, they can see it coming. The best thing is the way they talk to him, the one-to-one chat. Secondary schools need teachers who have got the training to cope with children like him.'

His mother

'I told her that she must tell me when things are going on at home. When she feels unsafe. She just needs to know people are there to chat to. Sometimes I don't see her for weeks then she's there every day if something goes wrong. She uses me to let off steam.'

A pastoral manager

Schools should be aware of some of the reasons why young people may not seek help. They include:

- fear of making the situation worse and causing angry recriminations
- embarrassment and awareness of the stigma attached to domestic violence
- fear of not being believed
- not knowing who to approach
- lack of access to a phone or knowledge of helplines
- fear of social services involvement.

The key adult might be responsible for the whole 'support package' around a young person and act as co-ordinator, where a number of agencies are involved.

How can schools make the time? Are staff really qualified? The wide-ranging roles of the key adult can be demanding, unpredictable, time-consuming and may not sit easily within a class teacher's responsibilities. It is difficult to be available at short notice or provide a regular time commitment. Yet school is where children are every day, where they have to cope. Arguably school staff, more than any other professionals, are in a position to make a difference.

In primary schools, key adults are often learning mentors, teaching assistants or senior teachers. In secondary schools, they might be learning mentors, behaviour support workers, teaching assistants, family support workers or year heads. A form tutor or class teacher may not be the ideal person, not only because of time issues but also because of potential role conflict.

It may take a young person a long time to feel secure enough to trust an adult with information that has been a long-standing secret. Often, a relationship will have gradually built up. Sometimes, a child will take the initiative and turn to a trusted adult out of the blue. It is important to listen and be available.

If a young person, and particularly an older child, is to be assigned a key adult, ideally they should have some choice in who this is; this is part of including them in decision making. Is there a particular person with whom they feel comfortable? Would that person be willing to take on a mentoring role?

Staff do not need to be trained counsellors (though obviously counselling training helps), but they will need certain skills and qualities. Below, we offer some advice and strategies for listening and helping children to talk.

Qualities of an effective key adult

The primary aim is to build a trusting relationship with the child. The key adult may also be proactive in getting to know the abused parent. Mothers have said how much they value the link with a key person in school.

Qualities in a key adult include an ability to be:

- calm, confident, and empathetic – a good listener
- patient and persistent
- hard to shock – able to cover up their own feelings and stay 'neutral'; not make value judgements
- reliable and consistent in their responses
- proactive – good at networking within and beyond school.

Other skills/attributes may include:

- experience of working with troubled children and young people
- an understanding of and ability to follow confidentiality guidelines
- an ability to handle disclosures with confidence and within child protection guidelines
- a good sense of humour.

The key adult might also be able to:

- notice aspects of school life that may be challenging; pick up on difficult times and days; suggest flexible arrangements and adjustments where appropriate
- intervene early on behalf of the child when things are becoming difficult
- act as an advocate for the child – with other teachers and in meetings
- co-ordinate a 'package of support' around the child
- work closely with teachers and other staff.

The role of key adult can be complex and stressful. It will work best when it is embedded in a positive school ethos, where staff are supported by processes and management. Effective supervision is vital. This means having time allocated with other professionals from within school or from external agencies. A key adult should feel supported and able to refer on, or signpost as appropriate.

Being available – the right time and space

'Children ... want to know that they will be listened to and their concerns will be taken seriously, so all education establishments should seek to demonstrate to children that they provide them with a safe environment where it is okay to talk.'

Department for Education and Skills 2006: 72

'You have to make them welcome. If you don't, they won't come. I'm here at 7.45. Some of the kids will come in early. It's important for them to know I'll be here. I make a point of being around at the end of school. I've had kids returning to see me. I let them know that if I'm not here, they can leave a message and I'll come and find them. You need a private space. Rooms full of learning mentors and other pupils are not appropriate.'

A family support worker

A pleasant space for a confidential chat is vital, yet often lacking in schools. Those involved in Building Schools for the Future, please take note! It can be unsettling for the young person and key adult to have to find a different 'corner' in which to talk each time they meet, and frequent interruptions are similarly disruptive. Visiting professionals also need a confidential space in which to see a child. Children need to feel comfortable if they are to begin to talk about their worries. Predictable places and routines reduce anxiety.

Note that some children may not need to see their key adult often, but find comfort in the knowledge that they are available when necessary. Others may meet up on a near daily basis.

'In this school, pupils talk more readily because of the ethos. We give a child a space to talk ... if they want to be quiet, they can stay quiet.'

A learning mentor

Some tips for key adults:

- try and be available at key times – before and after school, at breaks and lunchtimes

- let children know when you are available and how they can leave a message; children are unlikely to seek help from adults in a busy office
- consider designating times for pupil drop-ins
- be visible around school – give nods, acknowledgements, let the children know someone is looking out for them.

Building a relationship – developing rapport with a young person

'Children need to know they will not be judged; told they are right or wrong. It's looking at the situation together. Adults are not there to find solutions but to listen to the child and be a sounding board.'

A family support worker

Children rarely self-refer; often a member of staff, parent, or other professional will have suggested that a child sees a learning mentor or counsellor. How might a child feel? Some are told by a parent or carer not to talk to anyone about the home situation. Some think adults are not to be trusted; children may not be used to being listened to or having their views taken seriously. Anxious children carrying big secrets may not be easy to engage.

The role of key adults is not to solve problems or find solutions, but they can give young people opportunities to talk and be listened to actively, and provide them with language to express their feelings and opportunities to reflect on concerns they may never have raised before.

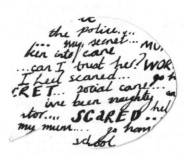

A key adult can:

- listen without judging
- acknowledge what the young person has been through or is going through and praise their coping strategies
- find out if they are feeling unsafe and address safety issues
- help the young person describe and make sense of how they are feeling and what they are thinking
- show the child that their thoughts and feelings matter
- do some joint problem solving with the child about what can help
- help the young person enjoy school life and achieve
- notice and celebrate small steps of progress, achievements and positive contributions to school life
- share fun, relaxing activities.

The key adult should be able to remain calm in challenging circumstances. A child may talk about terrifying events, either gradually or suddenly, and it can be difficult to suppress a shock response, but this is necessary if a child is to continue to feel they can talk openly.

> 'What they are talking about can be very shocking indeed but you haven't got to show them that, because as soon as you show that to people, the defences come up.'
>
> A learning mentor

Techniques for helping young people to talk

If staff think it would be helpful for a young person to meet regularly with a key adult to discuss emotional, pastoral and behavioural issues that could be related to domestic violence, the parent should be informed and consent obtained. Discussions should be confidential, except when it is necessary to adhere to child protection guidelines. So at the start, clarify:

- that the child knows why they are coming to see the key adult and agrees to the meeting
- what is already known, the source of the information and the young person's views on its accuracy
- confidentiality and the child's understanding of it. Explain that confidentiality can be kept, unless the child says something adults feel may present potential harm to them or to others, in which case information would have to be passed on (i.e. following child protection guidelines). If the key adult thinks it would be useful to share any other aspect of the discussion with another adult – a parent or teacher, for example – discuss this with the child and seek their agreement.

Other initial considerations should include:

- seating arrangements – sitting next to each other rather than opposite is often less threatening

How not to react

- offering biscuits and a drink – these are nurturing
- a predictable routine – where possible, the same room, same start time, same snack on offer
- establishing ways for the young person to indicate that the conversation is becoming uncomfortable. This gives them some control. It might be a picture of traffic lights, so that they can point to red (stop). It might be having feelings cards on the table – so they can point to how they are feeling, such as anxious or angry. (It may be necessary to clarify that the child can recognise and identify feelings.)

Some children will have difficulty expressing themselves through language – many will find direct conversation difficult – so be creative in finding other means of expression. Allow a child to lead their own play if this is what they want to do. Older children may enjoy play activities that are usually for younger children, so having plenty of toys can be helpful. Simple games like snakes and ladders, cards or Connect 4 can engage the child. Many children love attractive art and collage materials. Respond to the interests of the child.

> 'It's very hard for a child to sit face to face and talk about their problems, whereas, if you've got distraction methods, it takes the focus off them.'
>
> A domestic violence children's counsellor

Active listening – some tips

- Note the language the child uses to talk about their worries and use their words when reflecting back.
- Look for opportunities to praise, comment on how well they have coped, for being brave, caring and resourceful – things that help boost feelings of self-worth.

Some techniques for talking about feelings

Many young people who live or have lived with domestic violence feel anxious or unsafe. It can be helpful to explore fears and gauge the degree of distress. Some fears will be long-standing and affect the way the child thinks, feels and acts.

Children worry about their mothers being harmed and feel a great burden of responsibility. Primarily they fear further violence, but they may feel heightened anxiety about other things – their mother being run over or dying of cancer, for example. Some will also fear for their own safety and that of their siblings. They worry about continued disputes and about contact with the non-resident parent.

There may be recurring nightmares. Some of these fears will be realistic; others not. An adult in school will not be in a position to stop unpleasant things from happening; however, it should be possible to help a young person manage the fear and develop balanced views. An adult can support their thinking and understanding and help the child consider their own strengths and resilience.

The following are some strategies favoured by domestic violence children's counsellors. Their suitability will depend on the age, interests and level of understanding of the young person. Some techniques are taken from cognitive behavioural therapy. This aims to help people make the link between what they think, how this makes them feel and what they do about these thoughts and feelings. An excellent resource for working with anxious young people is *Think Good – Feel Good: A Cognitive Behaviour Therapy Workbook for Children and Young People* (Stallard 2003).

Worry bags

A worry bag helps children talk about their anxieties. It can give useful insight into their preoccupations. This activity is child-led, and so is uniquely relevant to their situation.

The child is asked to draw the outline of a bag and name the things that worry him or her. These worries are written on pieces of card and stuck onto the bag. The worries can then be examined individually. The child can be asked to rate each worry on a scale of 1 to 10, according to the level of anxiety it is causing.

Once a child has been able to name their anxieties, there can be some joint problem solving, as follows.

Examining the fear – What thoughts are going on in the young person's mind? What might end up happening? What is the worst thing that could happen?

Looking at the evidence – Is the concern realistic? (It may well be.) What is the evidence for and against it, for example, has it happened in the past? Is it possible or probable that it will happen again?

Safety concerns – Where these are real, the adult may be able to offer practical help or advice to the child or family in terms of safety planning (see examples below) or it may be appropriate to refer on.

A worry bag

Coping strategies – What are the young person's existing coping strategies? Are they helpful? What have they done so far? Are there any other ways of addressing negative thoughts and fears? Who are the child's supporters? If something unpleasant does happen, how will the young person cope? What is the young person already saying to himself or herself to address unhelpful anxieties?

Discussing trauma symptoms, e.g. nightmares, bedwetting, poor concentration – Young people can be informed that these symptoms are quite common in children who live with high levels of anxiety – we have nightmares when we have difficult feelings and worries; some children may hear or re-experience frightening incidents from the past.

This work can take place over several sessions and it may be helpful to refer to the worry bag at times. Then the bag should be put away and an enjoyable activity shared. Allowing the child to re-scale their worries in subsequent sessions provides the adult with the opportunity to monitor anxiety levels.

AN EXAMPLE OF THE WORRY BAG IN PRACTICE

Through his worry bag, a boy indicated extreme fear of and nightmares about his father breaking into the house and attacking his mother. On a thought thermometer (see below) he indicated a strong likelihood of this happening. He was also bedwetting. The child had devised a number of home-made solutions, such as leaving skates on the stairs in the hope that he could trip his father up. The counsellor related the fears to his mother, who considered them realistic and who herself was living in fear. The mother was then supported to contact the police domestic violence unit who made the house more secure with panic buttons and cameras. Once these things were in place, the boy's anxiety rating for this fear was reduced and work moved on to the next anxiety – about being seen by the father on the way to school.

Visual images

ANXIETY THERMOMETERS

A child can rate their current levels of anxiety using an anxiety thermometer. This can then be used as a monitoring device between sessions and a risk assessment tool.

THOUGHT THERMOMETERS

A child can show how strongly they hold a particular view or belief by using a thought thermometer.

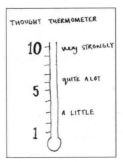

OTHER VISUAL IMAGES

A drawing of a kettle boiling over or a firework exploding can be used to identify triggers to a child's anger outbursts. What causes the kettle to boil over or the firework to explode?

Helping children to understand physiological responses to anger and anxiety

Children can be taught about the physical impact of anxiety or anger on their bodies. On an outline of a body, they can label bodily responses to high levels of agitation, e.g. tummy ache, tense muscles, blood rush to the head. This should help develop their awareness of signs of rising stress levels and support discussion about ways of reducing them and avoiding triggers.

There is a section on what happens to your body when you are angry or calm and useful worksheets in the book *A Solution Focused Approach to Anger Management with Children* (Stringer and Mall 1999).

Rating scales

Scales can be used to rate the strength and frequency of a feeling. Questions such as the following can be asked.

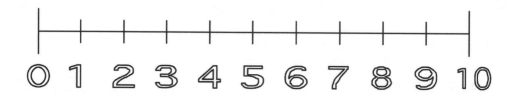

- Can you rate your fear/distress/anger on a scale of 0 to 10, where 0 is no distress at all and 10 is the worst it is possible to be?
- What would it take to lower the rating/temperature to …? What else? What else?*
- What are you already thinking/doing to stop the temperature rising to …? What else? What else?
- At what point on the scale would it be alright to be? Are there times when you are there? When is that?
- On a scale of 0 to 10, where 0 is never and 10 is always, how much of the time do you feel anxious/angry/sad/happy?

* The 'what else' question is very important. It encourages the young person to consider the range of possible strategies.

Celebrating success – building a positive self-image

Many young people feel they are in some way to blame for disharmony in their families and may carry shame and negative feelings about themselves. A key worker can help build a more positive self-image by highlighting and celebrating children's skills and strengths as well as their resourcefulness. Parents can be kept informed of positive steps through phone calls, certificates and praise postcards. Achievement books or good news books can be kept (resources on raising self-esteem are listed in Chapter 14).

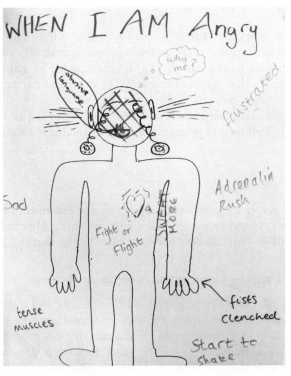

Feelings shoe boxes

A feelings shoe box is another way of helping young people to talk about their inner feelings. Ask children to cut out pictures and words from magazines that represent how they think they are seen by the outside world. Often people in magazines look happy, though they may just be putting on a brave face. Stick these on the outside of a shoe box. Inside, children can place pictures of facial expressions and words that represent their true feelings; the ones they keep to themselves. There can then be exploration of the children's thoughts, feelings and perceptions. This method is suitable for most children aged 10 or older.

Therapeutic board games

Therapeutic board games are games that are specifically designed to help young people explore feelings, beliefs and attitudes. Titles include Young Men and Violence Game, Peace Path, and Talk-It-Out (for details see the resources section in Chapter 14).

The football pitch – working towards goals, overcoming obstacles

An image of a football pitch can help children think about goal setting. The goal represents what the young person wants to achieve; the opposition represents the obstacles. The key adult can help identify the protective factors that can reduce the obstacles and therefore move the child towards the goal; together the adult and young person can then work their way towards the goal. There may be missed attempts at goal along the way but the aim is to help the young person reflect and move forward.

Ending sessions

It is good practice to summarise by going back to the beginning of the session and drawing out the main themes. It can be useful to ask for feedback; what does the young person think were the main points discussed? Has the session been useful? Some of the agreed strategies can be summarised for the young person and their understanding checked.

It may be difficult for the young person to go back to a lesson and settle after a talk, so consideration should be given to the timing of the end of the session. It may be advisable for a child to have access to a quiet place and a short break until the start of the next lesson. With the child's agreement, it may be helpful to relay some information to the parent or carer about the session; this may support positive and more open communication between them.

Note that if, during any of the above activities, a child makes a disclosure that may warrant social care referral, the session should be ended sensitively and the child informed about what the next steps will be. Staff should always follow local safeguarding procedures (see *Dealing with Disclosures*, below).

Referring on

The key adult may feel that the young person and/or the family have needs that require assessment and interventions from another professional or agency, either within or beyond school. This might be a social worker, Child and Adolescent Mental Health Service practitioner, specialist counsellor or educational psychologist. These concerns should be discussed with the parent and others in school; for example, the Special Educational Needs Co-ordinator, lead behaviour or pastoral professional. Parental consent for a referral should be obtained. Educational professionals should be aware of the circumstances under which it is appropriate to initiate a Common Assessment Framework (CAF) or make a child protection referral. The aim of the CAF is to help identify, at the earliest opportunity, unmet additional needs and provide co-ordinated support.

Safety planning

For children living with domestic violence, it may be appropriate to work to develop a safety plan to reduce the risk of harm in an emergency. Child protection procedures should also be followed. A useful start is to find what the young person is already doing to try and stay safe when domestic violence is happening. This is important; the child's strategy could actually be putting them at further risk. One child, for example, ran off when violence erupted in the house, sometimes taking a younger sibling along too. No one would know where he had gone.

Some children will have made some safer arrangements such as being at a friend's house when they suspect there might be a problem between their mother and her partner; others might go up to their room and put music on or play a computer game to remove themselves from the immediate situation.

Having explored what the child is doing already, the adult may work with him/her to draw up a safety plan. The Hideout website (http://www.thehideout.org.uk) has good guidance on this.

A safety plan might contain some or all of the following, depending on the individual child and their situation:

- the name of someone the child can confide in
- the name of a trusted person they can go to, who knows about the problem
- useful telephone numbers such as the police, Childline and people they can trust
- a rehearsal of what they might say if they do call the police
- a code word, so that if something happens they can call someone and follow a pre-agreed plan.

Consideration should also be given to how children can be supported during school holidays. Do they, for example, need helpline numbers, web sites and computer access?

For younger children and those with learning difficulties, the safety plan may be mainly pictorial.

One learning mentor did some group safety planning in her circle time sessions for upper Key Stage 2 pupils when pupils raised domestic violence issues. She used *What would you do if ...?* cards to discuss safety issues with groups.

A safe place to keep the plan should be discussed; it should not be kept in a schoolbag or under a pillow where it could be found by the abuser. Talking through whether or not the young person wants to share this plan with the abused parent is also helpful. This person may not be aware that their child knows about the domestic violence. It can be a difficult topic to broach as the child may feel they are just adding to the worries of a stressed parent.

Dealing with disclosures

The following guidance comes from *Safeguarding Children and Safer Recruitment in Education*:

> 'Any member of staff or volunteer who is approached by a child wanting to talk should listen positively and reassure the child. They should record the discussion with the pupil as soon as possible and take action in accordance with the establishment's child protection procedures. … If a child makes a disclosure to a member of staff, s/he should write a record of the conversation as soon as possible, distinguishing clearly between fact, observation, allegation and opinion, noting any action taken in cases of possible abuse and signing and dating the note.'
>
> Department for Education and Skills 2006: 73

Staff have a role in referring concerns on to children's social care; it is not their responsibility to investigate child protection concerns themselves. However, staff may be required to provide information for police investigations or enquiries under section 47 of the Children Act 1989. Local Safeguarding Children Boards have guidance for schools on managing a disclosure.

The following is good practice on how to respond when a pupil makes a disclosure:

- try and find somewhere quiet to talk
- keep calm, even if the child is revealing shocking information; let them know that you believe what they are telling you
- listen to them and use their terms – they may never have heard of 'domestic violence'
- let them know that what is happening is wrong and it is not their fault; it happens to lots of people and staff are there to try and help them be safer
- tell them that because it is wrong, you will have to talk to someone else about it, and explain why you can't keep complete confidentiality
- don't say that you can solve all their problems, but offer help and support – this might include offering information to the abused parent too, if appropriate
- if you need to find out more information for the child (e.g. some phone numbers), say so, and tell them that you will talk to them again
- end the session sensitively and let them know how they can contact you quickly if they want to.

Always follow the most recent government child protection guidelines.

Meeting the pastoral needs of young people affected by domestic violence

> 'The attitude of the individual teacher or teaching assistant is tremendously important. If your core belief is "I am here to teach and nobody should interfere with that right", then I think you are going to find working at a school like this extremely difficult … children will challenge you … Staff with an understanding of where

these children are coming from will do everything to talk calmly to the child and talk them down when they hit crisis point.'

The head teacher of a school near a women's refuge

Some parents who live with, or have recently fled, domestic abuse, may be too depressed, exhausted and caught up in their own difficulties to meet even their children's basic needs. (Some parents will not have the emotional resources for much positive engagement with their children.) It can be the norm for children to get themselves and younger siblings up, fed, and out in the morning. Most children need help with planning and organisation, as well as encouragement to participate fully in school life. If this is unavailable from home, adults in school may, in effect, need to step in.

Monitoring and support at the start of the day

Teachers frequently say you can tell as soon as a child walks in that it will be a bad day. Secondary teachers comment that they know when a child enters their lesson that there will be trouble. Consider the following:

* something may have happened in the family in the previous 24 hours that has distressed the child and impacted negatively on their mood or behaviour;
* the start of the day can be a time of heightened anxiety for a vulnerable child and the family. The daily separation from the abused parent can be distressing for children, so they may drag their feet about getting ready for school; getting out of the house can be very stressful;
* the child may have had a fraught journey to school. Some children and their carers may be in fear of an absent, abusive, parent;
* the child may be anxious because of homework not done, lack of uniform or equipment or another aspect of school.

Careful monitoring and appropriate support before the child enters the classroom may prevent the inevitability of behaviour outbursts later on. Some useful strategies include:

* have a key adult available for the handover from the mother. Some children may be comforted by a transitional object that reminds them of home, for example, a toy or a photograph;
* build in a short session with the key adult prior to the child entering the classroom. This is a way of monitoring well-being, checking the child is calm, has had breakfast, is in the right uniform and has the right equipment;
* when appropriate, provide calming activities, such as drawing or a short game, before the child enters the class;
* provide opportunities for the child to express things that have happened through drawing or in a journal before going to class;
* at secondary school, provide the young person with a locker or drawer within the Special Educational Needs/Inclusion department for schoolbooks and equipment. Staff may also keep a copy of the child's timetable and help the child prepare their bag for the day: ensure they have the right books and equipment; provide a note if

something is missing; check up on homework. In this way, staff are also modelling organisational skills;

- remind the child about what to do if things are getting too much to handle;
- remind the child about the availability and whereabouts of the key adult that day;
- go though the day's timetable (a visual timetable helps many children) and prepare the child;
- if the child is anxious about the safety of a parent or carer, help them by facilitating contact during the day – maybe via a phone call or text.

Worry/feelings boxes

Many primary classrooms now have worry or feelings boxes. By writing down their worries and putting the notes in the box, children can let their teacher know how they are feeling.

Breakfast and breakfast clubs

Children may come to school hungry and thirsty, so are unlikely to be able to learn effectively or behave well. Vulnerable children can be monitored before going to lessons and given the opportunity to take advantage of a supply of cereal and breadsticks. Many schools run breakfast clubs; a primary school head teacher ran one for both children and parents, so they could enjoy quality time at the start of the day – this can provide valuable respite for vulnerable families.

Homework clubs

Some children, particularly those in temporary accommodation, have nowhere calm or practical to do homework or are unable to access a computer. They should be given priority places at homework clubs and encouragement to attend. It is helpful to encourage attendance as part of their routine.

Supporting participation in extra-curricular activities and trips

Extra-curricular activities enrich a child's life and provide valuable experience of leisure time with good adult role models; a key adult can find out what is available, facilitate access, provide reminders and accompany the child if appropriate. Charges can be a barrier though Parent–Teacher Groups and voluntary agencies may be able to help.

A 'good news' book

A good news book documents a child's successes and is a permanent reminder of achievements. It should be a collection of positives and can include good work, positive comments, stickers, certificates, drawings, and photographs of the child. It can be shared with the child's family. There is no place in a good news book to record negative behaviour incidents. Those may need to be logged and reported to parents, but this should be done using another forum.

Planned arrangements for time-out

Children who have experienced turbulent events at home may yearn for a quiet space; somewhere simply to be, undisturbed by the hustle and bustle of school life and away from things that may trigger anxiety and behaviour outbursts. Young people from violent families have described their need for peace and quiet.

> 'Sometimes I wish I could be in a room on my own, no disturbances, just sitting down and doing my work.'
>
> A secondary school girl

> 'When I can't concentrate, I need somewhere to calm down ... To be alone to let my temper out.'
>
> A secondary school boy

Some schools have dedicated quiet spaces or 'places to be' for children who are finding it hard in class. Staff provide exit passes; sometimes with the aim of enabling a pupil to exit from a stressful situation before behaviour escalates. In schools that are proactive about pastoral care there is often nothing unusual about going to such a room. Children may sit and play, look at books, talk if they want to, calm down after a problem in a lesson. If pressure is not put on them, they are likely to relax because they are allowed some space and have a degree of control over the situation – something that may not happen very often outside school.

Some tips for time-out:

- adults and the child should be clear about the arrangements and how an exit pass should be used
- adults can help a child recognise when they may need some time-out. Trusted friends,

for example, in an empathetic group or a 'circle of friends', may also be able to help by suggesting time-out when they see their friend getting wound up

- when the child returns to class, it can be helpful for the teacher to give quiet acknowledgement; a smile or a comment about where the class is up to, positive affirmation, a welcome.

Supporting social interactions

Domestic violence adversely affects children's social relationships. Some children may appear passive, withdrawn or guarded about friendships. Others may be overly clingy and possessive. Many schools use a range of strategies and interventions to promote social integration and teach social skills; there are peer mentoring and buddying schemes and friendship benches in playgrounds. There are small-group circle time sessions and adult-structured interactive play sessions. Domestic violence children's workers have described the benefits of group work for vulnerable children. Most enjoy the chance to express themselves and be listened to in a safe environment. Small-group circle time activities can promote and enhance friendships and address issues that make children anxious. Such activities can address situations that young people find difficult both in and out of school. The *Quality Circle Time* books[1] written for pre-schoolers, primary and secondary children, are full of ideas for activities. There are also therapeutic board games such as *Socially Speaking* (see the resources section, Chapter 14).

A home–school book

Certain times can be particularly stressful for children and there may be a noticeable deterioration in behaviour. For example:

- immediately before and after contact visits
- around the times of court hearings
- when the family are moving house
- birthdays and Christmas; times when there may be uncertainty about contact.

A home–school book can be used to share such information and to support effective and regular two-way communication. It may be helpful to share information with other staff, with parental consent, on a 'need to know' basis.

Helping children with personal hygiene

Highly anxious or traumatised children may frequently wet or soil themselves. This can be distressing and embarrassing. A child may have wet a bed, or shared a bed with a sibling who has wet, and may not have showered and so will smell bad in school. This issue needs to be addressed quickly and sensitively as such a child is vulnerable to bullying. On a practical level, wipes, clean uniform and plastic bags for soiled clothing should be made available. A trusted key adult can also help the child understand that it is not their fault and make the link with their anxiety.

Times of transition and school moves

Changing schools and times of transition can be particularly difficult for vulnerable children who have enjoyed stability and security in a nurturing school and have developed close relationships with certain adults. The switch from primary school to the more complex secondary environment can also be a challenge.

Such transitions should be planned carefully. Ideally, a key adult should be identified early on to facilitate information sharing. There should be as much consistency and continuity of care as possible. Some secondary schools give vulnerable children opportunities for additional visits before starting, perhaps over a holiday when the corridors are empty.

New arrivals

It can be helpful to assign a key adult to a new pupil, maybe a learning mentor, who can get to know them and provide support and encouragement through the challenging early days. Some children may be out of the habit of attending school or may feel negative about it or reluctant. This year eight boy was excluded from his new school after a week:

> 'When I started, I didn't know any of the teachers. The form tutor was off with a broken leg, so we had someone different every day.'

Understanding behaviour and meeting needs

> 'I've about 30 children on my books, referred for behaviour or anger management difficulties, and I'd say at least half of them have got links to domestic violence. Teachers should understand these links. There needs to be some kind of awareness. Teachers aren't recognising them because it's something that isn't talked about.'
>
> A secondary school family support worker

When children are identified as having unexplained emotional and behavioural difficulties or where there are child protection concerns, schools should bear in mind that domestic violence may be an underlying factor as a significant number of these young people will come from families where domestic violence is present.

> 'When it came to light, staff gave much leeway. It was staff awareness that helped, not special treatment. He still needed to feel like everyone else.'
>
> A mother

It helps to view worrying or difficult behaviour in the light of home experiences. Some young people who live with high levels of stress may seem to be in a continual state of high arousal. Certain anxiety-driven behaviours can seem similar to those displayed by children with Attention-Deficit/Hyperactivity Disorder (AD/HD). Behaviour outbursts can result from anxiety that has gradually built up, and anger may conceal panic and terror. Outbursts can be triggered unwittingly by something that a child finds sensitive or threatening, such as being threatened by an authority figure, being asked to write about a sensitive topic or their mother being called names. It is frightening for a child to feel completely out of control, and humiliating when it happens in front of teachers and peers.

Where there are frequent outbursts, there should be careful recording and analysis of incidents. The A-B-C model may be useful to help staff identify triggers then make appropriate adjustments to support the child.

Antecedents – What was the context (day, time, seating arrangement, subject)? What was happening just before? What triggered the outburst?

Behaviour – Describe exactly what happened; the child's response.

Consequences – What did staff and the young person do?

Immediately after an outburst is not the time to do an analysis with a young person as they will need time to calm down. It is important not to add to their stress by asking why this has happened: they probably won't be able to say – or may genuinely not know or remember. It may be useful to establish the child's view – though if a child will not or cannot engage, there may be no point in going over the event. After a behaviour outburst, it is important to let the child know that he or she is welcome back in the class.

> 'These kids ... the last thing they need is somebody to be shouting at them. There's no point. What tends to happen is they kick off and you shout. It's not going to improve anything. It's just going nowhere, is it? For many, it's just what they've been through for years.'
>
> A family support worker

Vulnerable children will do better in a calm and orderly classroom. Other management strategies are similar to those used for children with AD/HD. They might include:

- giving careful thought to seating arrangements – near an adult; away from distractions
- minimising waiting or unstructured time, e.g. at the start of lessons; when a child has their hand up
- 'kick-starting' the child with work, once it has been explained to the class
- breaking tasks into small chunks with frequent monitoring and feedback
- giving the child preferential access to computers, maybe with headphones to aid concentration. Some software provides immediate feedback, so children are not kept waiting
- giving lots of attention to positives and appropriate behaviour; highlighting what they are doing right.

It is helpful to include children in finding solutions by finding out what helps and what is happening when things are going well. Ask about what helps them to stay calm and what 'presses their buttons'. Ask what or who can help if they are worked up or angry.

Other helpful strategies include:

- providing a calm place where the child can shut off – this could be a quiet corner with activities such as a CD player and headphones, books, magazines, or a computer activity
- having a box of calming activities to hand – Lego, colouring, sorting and matching games (for younger children)
- providing a stress ball, toy, or piece of Blu Tack or Play-Doh to fiddle with, squeeze or poke
- agreeing with a child in advance to trust a particular signal from an adult that time-out is needed.

Children whose behaviour can challenge staff

'She knows how to intimidate teachers. She knows what she's doing is wrong, but that's her coping mechanism. She needs to get in there first before they hurt her. She's jumping in quickly instead of dealing with it in a different way.'

A family support worker

Children who have lived with domestic abuse are more likely than others to respond aggressively and on impulse when under threat, to perceive hostile intent, feel picked on and feel that they are being given dirty looks. They are more likely to fly off the handle. Domestic violence within a family provides a negative model of conflict resolution and anger management.

Young people may benefit from opportunities to reflect on their negative experiences and on how past events may have shaped the way they react to things. Anger can be explored with whole classes, small groups or individuals. Some schools provide anger management courses. Many children will see anger as a bad emotion that they shouldn't have. There are books written for younger children who feel angry (see Chapter 14, resources section) that can be used with a group. Children who have lived with abuse will have good reasons for being angry, but need help to understand that aggression and intimidation are not appropriate ways of dealing with conflict. Role models such as Martin Luther King can exemplify positive ways of dealing with unjust situations. A good therapeutic tool is *Helping Children Locked in Rage or Hate* (Sunderland and Hancock 1999), in which there are sections on trauma and on helping the child to make sense of why they are behaving as they are.

Given that a key element of domestic violence is power and control in relationships, intervention work should cover healthy and respectful interactions, relationships and conflict resolution. This will be discussed further in Chapter 14.

A mediating role for a key adult

It is challenging for any teacher to have a young person in class who is disruptive, aggressive, hostile or volatile. It can help if teachers understand some of the underlying reasons for this behaviour and for the young person to know that the teacher has some insight into their difficulties.

'Sharing information needs to be handled in a sensitive way; safety and confidentiality issues are paramount. Yet if some information is shared, it can make the child's life a bit better when they're in the classroom or on the corridors.'

A family support worker

The family support worker quoted above offers to mediate between a child and teachers with whom there is a precarious relationship. An agreement is made beforehand as to what parts of the child's 'story' can be discussed, and the issues the child would like raised. This is done in an informal and relaxed way.

'If a child has had a few bad lessons, he'll go in thinking he'll have another one. We can offer a way of intervening – and it works. You have to do it with the child and the teacher there, so they can both acknowledge each other's issues and they can resolve it together. By the end of the session they can be laughing together. The child has gone back and there's been no more atmosphere. They are greeted in a friendly way; maybe the teacher feels they can let their guard down a bit. So the teacher's not going to immediately get their back up, the child is not going to be kicking off within minutes. They've moved on. We've done this with some of my more difficult ones who have been referred for anger management.'

Extreme reactions to authority figures

Some children may have often experienced adults as being frightening and controlling. They may also have internalised that authority figures – such as the police or social workers – do drastic things and impose significant changes. Such children may then react in an extreme way to the threat of an authority figure such as the head teacher.

When a person feels under threat, adrenalin rises and the body reacts in a certain way. The nervous system gets ready for action. In primitive times, if a caveman was confronted with a sabre-toothed tiger, he would do one of three things:

- fight back
- take flight (run away)
- freeze (play dead).

Our physiological response to threat has not changed. In school, if a child is threatened, for example, with a visit to the head teacher, that threat can provoke a panic reaction. There may be a fight, flight or freeze response: aggression, running away, or sudden compliance. It will be helpful for staff to notice and record extreme responses to particular threats so appropriate management strategies can be planned.

Children who seem prone to lying and exaggeration

'We know children can sometimes have magical thinking or distorted thinking. It's our job to support them with that. It's about going along with it at this point in time, not dismissing their thought processes.'

Domestic violence children's counsellor

Young people may give rambling accounts of what has happened in their lives and these can tip into fiction. It may be helpful to let the child know that sometimes it is normal for children who have lived through distressing events to have imaginary pictures in their mind, and these can sometimes be frightening.

Use of restraint – a word of caution

Children from violent and abusive backgrounds may react to restraint or so-called 'positive handling' in an extremely negative way. They may panic if adults try to get hold of them. One boy described how a behaviour incident had escalated to the point where he had tried to run away (in physiological terms, the flight response, referred to above). When adults tried to restrain him, he kicked off violently (a fight response). A child who has been abused may react very strongly if he or she feels closed in and unable to escape. Schools should consult Department for Children, Schools and Families guidance about the use of force to control or restrain pupils.

Exclusions and sending pupils home

During the school day, some children who live with domestic violence will have a strong desire to return home to check things are alright. If a child knows that disruptive behaviour will result in their being sent home, then there is a rationale to being disruptive. It will be more helpful in the long run for school to have a place where the child can have some time-out; summoning a parent should be a last resort because this can, in effect, reward disruptive behaviour.

School can be one of the only stable and consistent factors in the lives of children from chaotic families, many of whom will already have experienced significant loss and rejection. Troubled children need routine and predictability and may be vulnerable when not in school. Reduced timetables and fixed-term exclusions are sometimes used when children are struggling to cope. However, such strategies can compound the difficulties of the child and the family and add to the mother's stress. Parents have described how:

- young people soon get out of routine, have little structure to their day and stay awake at night, often spending long unsupervised hours on computer games or the internet
- their own jobs can be put at risk because they have to stay at home with the child
- their children meet other excluded children during school hours and can risk getting into trouble.

In addition, when excluded from school and left unsupervised, young people are at greater risk of abuse from strangers and the abuser. They are more susceptible to risk-taking behaviour, such as taking alcohol and drugs, and to sexual exploitation.

When a young person's behaviour is such that they are at risk of exclusion, it is essential that all agencies work together to maintain the placement.

Challenging the notion of a 'cycle of violence' in families

A key message for staff and parents to give to young people, and in particular to boys, is that growing up with domestic violence does not mean a young person is destined for violent relationships in adult life, either as an abuser or a victim. In fact, many children and young people will be determined never to abuse when they are adults, and never do.

Unfortunately, parents and other figures of authority may fall into the trap of making comparisons between an angry child and a violent parent. For example, in a refuge, a mother kept telling her son he was 'just like his dad', while speaking negatively about his dad within his hearing. Children may be labelled as controlling, aggressive and bad, and these labels can come to define them. If the labels are repeatedly reinforced by authority figures, young people can become locked into this view of themselves; the labels can become part of their identity. Young people may feel they have no control over their anger and aggression, that it is part of them, and that the cycle of violence is inevitable.

In Saunders (1995: 11) a man described his feelings of the 'inevitability' of a violent future as one of the most disabling and paralysing feelings he had experienced.

> 'After I had my son, I became obsessed with my violent background. I just had to know about my dad. I was convinced that because he had been violent, I would also be violent to my son. It's a terrible burden to have to live with, and which despite everything you know to be true never quite seems to go away.'

Adults should:

- take care not to label young people as controlling, aggressive, manipulative or violent;
- avoid making comparisons between the young person and a violent family member. School staff should stress the importance of this to mothers;
- reinforce the fact that there is no inevitability about young people who have lived with domestic violence becoming violent adults (both individually and in group teaching);
- help children understand more about why domestic violence happens in families; help individuals understand the history and context of their own situation.

> 'Children need to understand they don't have to end up like their parents. They need to understand what makes their parents like that.'
>
> A mother

During individual sessions, an adult can help a young person deconstruct 'negative' labels, and provide a counter-balance. A useful resource to address this can be found in *A Solution Focused Approach to Anger Management with Children* (Stringer and Mall 1999). A child can be helped to replace negative self-perceptions and labels with a different and more positive picture. A supporting adult can find out more about the young person's values and how they fit in with his or her hopes for the future. There can be discussion about the young person's strengths and skills – and a record made of these. Positive comments from friends and members of staff can be invited and evidence of alternative views found and presented to the child. A skills and achievements folder can be compiled.

The rap below exemplifies the therapeutic value of poetry writing. It helped a young person who witnessed domestic violence process his experiences. Its author now leads a productive life.

Domestic Violence

I don't understand why dem girl get beaten,
in my heart I feel dats not a nice way to treat em,
when there gone u just wanna go out 'n' meet em.

So they come back then for a day n walk out again
cos they've just got beaten.
Den u meet em again wiv a box of chocolates n some flowers.
So when de come back u can unleash da fury n da power.

So u just don't wanna treat em u jus wanna beat em.

So what is dis life dat we're livin
all da pain to da women dat these men are giving.
Leaving em to struggle wiv no food for da kids, no money now.
Don't laugh cos dis business aint funny!

Written by K.I.D. Published with kind permission

Responding to young people at risk of a forced marriage

Research suggests some schools are reluctant to tackle forced marriage issues openly for fear of upsetting parents or the local community; for example, some schools have been reluctant to display posters with helplines (House of Commons, Home Affairs Committee 2008). The government has published multi-agency statutory guidance (HM Government 2008), downloadable from http://www.fco.gov.uk/forcedmarriage.

The guidance states that senior managers should ensure that:

- forced marriage is automatically handled as a child protection issue;
- staff have appropriate training in order to understand the importance of sharing information with other agencies at the earliest opportunity to safeguard children and young people from significant harm or to prevent a crime being committed;
- staff share information promptly when a child or young person is at risk of forced marriage;
- staff provide information to the Forced Marriage Unit;
- staff understand the difference between breaking confidence (involving the child or young person's family without consent) and sharing information with consent with other appropriate professionals to prevent the child or young person being at risk of significant harm.

HM Government 2008: 24

Marriage:
It's YOUR choice

Marriage is something that most of us dream of happening... one day. But for some people, marriage can become a nightmare – when they're forced to marry someone against their will.

Forced marriage is wrong.
If this is happening to you, or someone you know, this is not your fault and you are not alone.

YOU CAN GET HELP.

→ Talk about your concerns to your teacher or ....

→ Call the Forced Marriage Unit on 020 7008 0151 between 9am and 5pm Monday to Friday (UK time). Outside those hours, call 020 7008 1500 and ask for the Foreign Office Response Centre.

→ Email fmu@fco.gov.uk

We offer confidential help and advice: we will **not** contact your family

→ For more information go to www.fco.gov.uk/forcedmarriage
If you are in immediate danger of harm or being taken abroad against your will, call the police on 999.

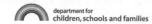

department for
children, schools and families

With kind permission from the Department for Children, Schools and Families, reproduced under the terms of the Click-Use Licence.

Downloadable from the web site http://www.dcsf.gov.uk/everychildmatters/resources-and-practice/IG00331/

'Every Child Matters' guidance states:

> 'If there are concerns that a child (male or female) is in danger of a forced marriage, local agencies and professionals should contact the Forced Marriage Unit (FMU), where experienced caseworkers are able to offer support and guidance, by calling 020 7008 0151 or by visiting the FMU page of the Foreign and Commonwealth Office website. The police and children's social care should also be contacted.'
>
> http://www.everychildmatters.gov.uk/socialcare/
> safeguarding/forcedmarriage/

Schools should be aware of guidance published by the Foreign and Commonwealth Office and Department for Education and Skills *Dealing with Cases of Forced Marriage: Guidance for Education Professionals* (2005),[2] available at http://www.everychildmatters.gov.uk/_files/FMarriageGuidanceEducation.pdf

The guidance lists the following warning signs:

- a sudden drop in performance due to feeling 'What's the point? I'll be married next year'
- truancy from lessons – it provides an escape from virtual imprisonment at home
- conflicts with parents over continued or further education
- excessive parental restrictions and control
- history of domestic violence within the family
- extended absence through sickness or overseas commitments
- depressive behaviour including self-harming
- history of older siblings leaving education early and marrying early.

> (See also *Warning signs of a victim of forced marriage*
> in HM Government 2008: 15.)

All staff should bear in mind that mediation as a response to forced marriage can be dangerous and place a young person at risk. Refusal to go through with a forced marriage has, in the past, been linked to so-called 'honour crimes'.

> 'In cases of forced marriage discussion with the family or any involvement of the family or local community members will often place the child or young person at greater risk of harm.'
>
> HM Government 2008: 21

School policies and a member of staff with responsibility for domestic violence issues

All schools have a teacher with responsibility for safeguarding children, but this teacher may not have been specifically trained to respond to domestic violence and forced marriage issues (House of Commons, Home Affairs Committee 2008). This report recommends that:

> 'specific accredited training be introduced for all education professionals on these issues ... In the first place, this could amount to ensuring that a designated contact for domestic violence and forced marriage exists in each school.'

Statements acknowledging the negative impact of domestic violence and outlining relevant strategies to address it should be included in a school's policy documents, for example, on behaviour, attendance and punctuality, personal, social and religious education, citizenship, child protection and exclusion.

Summary

School staff can improve the life chances of children who have experienced domestic violence, and have a positive effect on each of the five outcomes in the Every Child Matters programme. Of all professionals working with young people, school staff may be best placed to pick up on signs of distress and to respond to the needs of the child.

This chapter highlighted the need for training so that staff can pick up on children's warning signs and understand the barriers they face to education. Young people want to be able to seek support from adults in school; parents want staff to understand and support their children.

Key points from this chapter are as follows.

- Young people want access to adults who listen, take their concerns seriously, involve them in decisions and in finding solutions and consult them about possible outcomes (Mullender *et al.* 2002).
- Having a relationship with one key, trusted adult in school who can share a child's anxieties, provide emotional and behavioural support and monitor feelings of safety and well-being can make a big difference and sometimes be key to maintaining a child's school place.
- In order to learn and gain positive experiences from school, young people need to feel safe. Adults may be able to identify when this is not the case and refer on or offer support as appropriate.
- Domestic violence raises child protection issues and staff should be familiar with the school's child protection procedures; they should understand that they cannot guarantee confidentiality to a child.
- Sometimes, when families are in crisis, staff will need to step in and provide some of the basic pastoral care usually expected of a parent or carer.
- Working with the parent or carer can often be the key to effective work with children.

Notes

1 Mosley, J and Tew, M (1999) *Quality Circle Time in the Secondary School: A Handbook of Good Practice*. London: Fulton; and Mosley, J (1998) *Quality Circle Time in the Primary Classroom*. Cambridge: LDA.

2 Foreign and Commonwealth Office (2005) *Dealing with Cases of Forced Marriage: Guidance for Education Professionals*. Ref FCO 75263 (2005). FCO: London.

Chapter 11

The roles of other professionals

A number of professionals can support children and families who are adversely affected by domestic violence. Sometimes a school or pre-school may make a referral to request their services. Sometimes professionals may contact schools to exchange information. Some may be able to provide advice, support and training to school staff. There are regional variations in provision, so schools should familiarise themselves with their own local services.

Child and Adolescent Mental Health Services (CAMHS)

CAMHS are part of the National Health Service (NHS) and provide mental health services for children, young people and families. Teams usually consist of child psychiatrists, clinical psychologists, psychiatric nurses and other child mental health professionals, including staff from social care. They may be hospital or community based. CAMHS professionals may assess, diagnose and support or treat young people experiencing mental health problems, where domestic violence and other child abuse is or has been a factor. The children's conditions may include anxiety, trauma and behaviour disorders. Often schools can refer children directly, though parental consent will be needed.

The Royal College of Psychiatrists provides information on a range of mental health issues on its web site, including leaflets on parenting and domestic violence, see http://www.rcpsych.ac.uk

Educational psychologists

Educational psychologists work with children who have complex learning, behavioural or emotional needs. Most education settings have a designated educational psychologist, who may provide:

- psychological assessment of a young person whose behavioural, learning and emotional well-being may be adversely affected by living with domestic violence
- consultation and advice to staff who teach and work with the young person
- individual support and therapeutic interventions
- statutory assessments that contribute to statements of Special Educational Needs
- liaison with other agencies, such as counselling services, social care, CAMHS.

Social care

Children's social care services seek to promote the well-being of children in need and looked-after children. They provide a range of care and support services for children and families, including families where children are assessed as being in need (including disabled children), children who may be suffering 'significant harm' and children who require looking after by the local authority (through fostering or residential care). See http://www.everychildmatters.gov.uk/socialcare/socialservices/

Safeguarding and promoting the welfare of children

A social worker has lead responsibility for undertaking an assessment of the child's needs and the parents' capacity to respond appropriately within their wider family and environment. This may involve contacting school as part of the information-gathering process. One in three child protection cases shows a history of domestic violence to the mother (Department for Education and Skills 2006: 74).

Social services are responsible for co-ordinating an inter-agency plan to safeguard the child, which sets out and draws upon the contribution of family members, professionals and other agencies, including schools.

Domestic violence counsellors and support workers

Schools may be able to access children's counsellors and support workers who are specialists in domestic violence issues. Schools may make enquiries through the Local Safeguarding Children Board, the local Domestic Violence Forum, the Children's Society, the NSPCC, Barnardos, Childline, Women's Aid and CAMHS. Workers may:

- provide counselling to children in schools, children's or family centres or at other venues
- provide support groups for young people
- provide training for school staff on domestic violence issues.

Local Safeguarding Children Board (LSCB) trainers

Staff of LSCBs provide comprehensive multi-agency training for professionals working with children, including school staff, to safeguard vulnerable children. This will include training on domestic violence and its impact on children.

Refuge children's workers

Most refuges employ children's workers. They have a key role in developing links with local schools, helping families find school places and communicating with schools about a child's educational and pastoral needs. They may:

- work to support children's transitions and settle children into new schools when they have had to move because of domestic violence
- support mothers with parenting

- provide support and social activities for children and parents affected by domestic violence.

Domestic violence forums

Domestic violence forums exist in most areas of the country. They may include representatives from the police, social care, housing, education, the legal profession, the voluntary sector and Women's Aid, who work together to tackle domestic violence issues.

School Attendance Improvement Service

School Attendance Improvement Service officers provide advice and support to schools and parents on matters relating to attendance. Domestic violence often underlies poor school attendance so officers are likely to work with children and families affected by it. They may:

- provide support to parents/carers to help support their children's attendance
- work with a pupil or parent, at home or in school, on the causes of attendance difficulties; encourage a return to school and support home–school communication
- signpost parents to support groups or parenting programmes
- inform parents of their legal responsibilities
- alert appropriate staff in a school's senior leadership team to possible child protection issues.

School Health Advisors

School Health Advisors aim to promote and maintain pupils' health and well-being; they may be aware that children are in families where there is domestic violence. They may:

- see pupils in confidence about physical or mental health issues, that could include domestic violence
- take appropriate steps to safeguard children and young people and liaise with other professionals when appropriate.

Parent Partnership Services

Parent Partnerships are statutory services that offer information, advice and support to the parents and carers of children with special educational needs (SEN). They operate at arm's length from the local authority and their work is impartial. Whilst the focus is on school, much work takes place through home visits. Some workers develop a relationship over time with the parents of a child with SEN; the issue of domestic violence and the impact it has had on their child or children is sometimes raised. Some parents may seek support to access counselling and psychological services. See http://www.parentpartnership.org.uk

Parent Partnership workers may:

- meet with parents/carers to discuss concerns about their children's SEN and inclusion

- help with form filling and letter writing
- support parents/carers with requests for meetings and provide support at meetings; support appeals
- support parents whose children have been bullied or excluded.

Connexions partnerships

Connexions Services bring together the key youth support services. Local authorities are responsible for their delivery. For local information, see http://www.connexions-direct.com and click on Local Services.

Personal advisors offer information and guidance for 13- to 19-year-olds on education, training, employment, and issues such as health, relationships, family and rights. Young people can talk in confidence and independently of home, family and school. Where domestic violence is an issue, personal advisors can listen to young people and signpost them to other services. They will act appropriately so as to safeguard young people.

Housing departments

Housing staff may become aware of domestic violence issues when working with homeless families or those at risk of becoming homeless. Where domestic violence is identified, the safety of children must be considered in any offer of accommodation. Housing staff may also be involved in Common Assessment Framework meetings around vulnerable pupils in schools.

Chapter 12

Supporting transient pupils and those in refuges and temporary accommodation

'The children arrive with nothing; they have left their friends, their school, sometimes their siblings, other family members and toys. The children are shell-shocked, especially the older ones. So either they are quiet or there are externalising behaviours.'

A head teacher

'Schools should develop protocol focusing on the special needs/requirements of vulnerable children attending from a refuge environment.'

Department for Education and Skills 2006: 74

'It is important that effective systems are in place to ensure that children from homeless families receive services from health and education ... because these families move regularly and may be at risk of becoming disengaged from services.'

HM Government 2006: 209

In Part 1, we outlined particular difficulties faced by children in refuges and temporary accommodation, including:

- many attend several schools and miss out on education
- records can be incomplete or missing
- some will arrive at a new school stressed or traumatised
- some will have considerable additional educational needs.

In this chapter, ways that schools can support this vulnerable group are described. We consider:

- admissions: obtaining records and background information, assessing needs and welcoming children
- providing emotional support
- providing practical help, including giving consideration to immediate safety and confidentiality issues
- finding a school place.

Admissions

> 'Children need to be in school as quickly as possible. They need to get back to a stable routine. Traumatised children need to be back with others.'
>
> A head teacher

Many refuges have well-established links with their local schools. Refuge staff value schools where professionals have an understanding of the particular difficulties faced by children living in refuges. They like being able to recommend schools, with confidence, to mothers. They particularly value:

- schools that admit children quickly and possibly without paperwork
- a strong ethos of caring and welcoming, with a unified approach from staff to supporting and nurturing children
- staff who understand confidentiality and safety issues
- support with entitlements such as free school meals
- staff who understand the difficulties and possible stigma attached to living in temporary accommodation.

The first port of call for a new arrival is often the school office. Staff there should have some training about issues facing families fleeing domestic abuse, including an understanding of why some parents may be unable to provide documentation such as birth certificates and benefit books. These, needed for proof of eligibility for free school meals, are often left behind when the family flee, or can be mislaid in transit.

Assessing the needs of new arrivals

> 'With most transient families, records are missing. We can contact the last school, but often it's like a jigsaw. Some children will only stay for a few days; some arrive with statements but the support is difficult to arrange, especially if it's unlikely the family will stay.'
>
> A head teacher

Obtaining the education records of transient children can be complex and time consuming. Some attend several schools within a short space of time; records may not keep up with the child and can be out of date or incomplete.

It will help if the school can gather a coherent history of a young person's education and significant home experiences from the parent. It should then be easier to backtrack to previous schools and obtain relevant information to establish a plan to meet the child's needs.

The admission should be conducted sensitively, with time and a quiet place allocated for a senior member of staff to sit down with the mother. Confidentiality issues can also be discussed.

> 'At the interview, we ask parents to be open, honest and tell us any issues relevant to

schooling. It helps if we know as much as possible. C.'s mum was keen to talk about the difficulties with her dad.'

A senior teacher

'I would say to a parent if there are issues at home affecting a child, then school need to know. If the parent is not getting help, I will put them in touch with agencies or contact agencies on their behalf. It's very rare parents don't want school to know.'

A head teacher

'I didn't want them to take pity. But it was better for the kids and me that they all knew. They'd know why my son was like he was, from what he'd been through. That's what helped me. They seemed to understand me.'

A mother

The following enquiry list may be helpful:

- names and details of previous schools attended, for however short a time
- attendance history
- details of home moves. Were these crisis moves?
- current home circumstances and reasons for the latest move. Is there likely to be another move in the near future?
- details of prolonged absence from education, with dates where possible
- any significant separations and losses experienced by the child
- additional learning or behaviour needs identified by previous schools. Has the child needed additional learning or behaviour support? Is there a statement of special educational needs?
- details of previous professional involvement, e.g. social workers, school attendance officers, educational psychologists, learning or behaviour support services, speech and language therapists, counselling services. Can the names of individuals or organisations be provided?
- does the parent have concerns about learning or behaviour?
- has the child been in situations that have been particularly distressing?
- are there any safety issues relating to the child? Are there any threats from an ex-partner?
- are there any concerns about getting to and from school, e.g. funding for transport, concerns about safety?
- details of siblings (resident and non-resident). Does the child have any caring responsibilities?
- who has parental responsibility for the child? Are there any legal orders in force? Is there anything school needs to know about access and contact arrangements?
- are any court cases pending?

The transfer of school records

The School Admissions Code (Department for Children, Schools and Families 2008b: para 3.49) states the following:

'When a child moves from one school to another in England, the school that the child moves from **must** transfer their educational record to the new school no later than 15 school days after the child ceases to be registered there. Where the school does not know which school the child has transferred to, and it is not reasonably practicable for it to find out ... it **should** send a common transfer file for that pupil via the Secure Data Transfer (S2S) web site http://www.teachernet.gov.uk/S2S identifying the destination school as 'unknown'. This information is then stored in the Lost Pupil Database. Schools which do not receive common transfer files for new pupils can ask local authority contacts to search this database to see if the files are there.'

ContactPoint

From 2009, ContactPoint, the new national index for children, will be another way for authorised staff to find out about what professionals are involved with the young person and who to contact. This should make it easier to deliver more co-ordinated support. It is a basic online directory and a key part of the Every Child Matters programme. Note that a system of shielding records will be in place when the disclosure of a child's address may put the family at risk, e.g. because of domestic violence. Access to records will be restricted to key individuals. See http://www.ecm.gov.uk/contactpoint

Providing emotional support

Welcoming new children

A child's admission should be planned carefully. Prior to starting, young people will appreciate a welcoming visit with the comfort of their mother by their side. For children known to have learning, emotional or behavioural difficulties, it may be helpful to arrange a multi-agency meeting as quickly as possible to plan for their needs.

'On admission to the school, these children are not just normal new starters. They need to feel straight away that they belong. Little things that require thought rather than time can make all the difference in terms of promoting that feeling.'

A head teacher

'We are the local school for the refuge. We try and make people feel wanted. There are similar issues with asylum seekers. Children are greeted, met and supported by other children. We are known as the caring school. Support is in place for all vulnerable children.'

A head teacher

Promoting feelings of safety and belonging

* Staff should ensure they can pronounce and spell children's names correctly.
* Siblings should be told of each other's whereabouts in school; they are often anxious about each other. One head allowed older siblings to stay with the younger ones until they felt comfortable. Siblings may wish to meet up at breaks and lunchtime.
* Ensure children know the arrangements for the end of the day; where to wait and

who to see if they are anxious.

- Ensure that a child's name is on their peg, that they have a tray with their name on and a book bag, like the other children, right from the start. In secondary school, ensure names are on all tutor lists.
- Wearing the correct uniform is key to belonging. Schools should keep a stock of clean uniforms. With second-hand clothes, ensure the name of the previous owner has been removed and that the child's name is put in.
- Organise a buddy. It can be helpful to select a child who is playing a full part in the life of the school.
- Plan the first few playtimes and help to structure social opportunities, because children who have moved frequently may no longer be willing to 'invest' in settling and establishing new friends: a protective strategy to avoid the pain of separation.

Pre-empt difficult or embarrassing questions

'So where are you from and where do you live?' A child who is unprepared for these questions and who has just moved to a refuge can be at a loss as to how to respond. For security and out of embarrassment, a young person may not wish to give a straight answer. Children can be helped to prepare a response with which they feel comfortable; refuge workers may also offer advice on this. Children might say they are living with friends or an aunty. Some children may be seen coming out of the refuge in the morning, so they could say it's a hotel or a flat until their new house is ready. In some circumstances, schools have agreed that the child can arrive late to ensure they are not seen coming out of the refuge.

Avoid putting pressure on children or their parents or carers

When a family is known to be under significant stress, teaching staff should not place academic or homework pressure on the children. School work will be of secondary importance (though for some children, it is a welcome escape). Staff should also avoid putting pressure on parents who are struggling to cope.

> 'I do his homework, he can't do it. He gets upset about it. It's a source of stress and he gets upset if he gets it wrong. I don't want him to miss out on playtime.'
>
> A mother

> 'I was made to feel I was a useless mother for not listening to the kids read as often as I should. They told me off about the state of his shirt.'
>
> A mother

Be aware of sensitive topics

Children can be highly sensitive about family breakdown and the stigma of being in temporary accommodation. Staff should try and avoid placing them in difficult situations.

> 'One little boy had been in the refuge over the summer holidays. The first writing task at his new school was about the holidays. Well he kicked off; he was so ashamed

about being in a refuge and that was how he knew he could get out of it. That was a terrible start for him. His mechanism for getting out of things was to kick off and be removed from the classroom.'

A refuge children's worker

Where there are potentially sensitive topics, children could be given choices of activity, for example, they could be asked to write about the summer holidays *or* what they are looking forward to this term.

Helping young people retain a sense of control

Young people who have had to leave their home and school can feel as though they have lost all control over their lives and no longer know or have a say in what is happening. Adults can help by keeping them informed and involved in some decisions, both in school and out of school, so they can make sense of events and retain a sense of control. Young people need to feel that their opinions count and are valued. In school, where appropriate, they should be encouraged to contribute to meetings and decisions that concern them. This may be by attending the meeting or by giving their views to an adult who will attend.

'Sometimes the young person gets called in after the behaviour or pastoral support plan has been devised and is told, "We've been talking and this is what you'll do". It's so important that they are given a say.'

A children's counsellor

Children who are anxious about their mother's well-being

Some children will be afraid to leave their mother in the refuge, due to fear for her safety while they are at school. Schools could arrange some contact for such children during the day – a phone call or a text, for example.

Social arrangements

When young people are making new friendships, they might want to meet after school at one another's houses. Adults can help try to pre-empt potentially difficult situations. For example, their mother could take the children out for a burger rather than friends coming to the house for tea or a play.

Practical help

Free school meals

Refuge children's workers cited cases where children have been prevented from starting school because there was no money for a school meal. It may take a number of days or weeks to get benefits in place because of missing documents. To overcome this, staff in one refuge reported that some schools and local authorities were willing to be flexible and accepted letters from refuges as proof of entitlement.

Help with transport and transport costs

Families may need help with transport costs. Children may have moved out of the area but still attend their old school or they may be at a new school, which is not within walking distance of their accommodation. For safety reasons, they may have to travel by taxi. Schools should contact the local authority about their transport policy and any help that is available.

Safety and confidentiality issues

'The main reason I chose this school was because outsiders could not see into the playground.'

A mother, having fled a violent partner

All staff should understand the safety and confidentiality issues that affect families fleeing violence because abusers can be persistent in trying to trace former partners and children. The following should be noted:

- if someone phones asking whether children attend the school, this should be neither confirmed nor denied. No information about children should be given over the phone
- staff should be aware of who collects the child from school. Some mothers may prefer it if children are allowed to wait to be collected indoors and out of sight
- if a child moves on to another school, the previous school should never pass on information about where they have gone
- staff should be aware that photographs of school events in the local paper that happen to feature children who have fled violence could give their whereabouts away
- it is useful to know who has parental responsibility. This can be complex; if it is unclear, advise the parent to seek legal advice; the Cafcass web site may be a good starting point, see http://www.cafcass.gov.uk. Legal advice may be available from the Citizens Advice Bureau, see http://www.citizensadvice.org.uk
- the school should be aware of any legal orders in force
- school staff should be aware that refuges provide all outside contacts, including schools and local authorities, with PO box addresses only, in order to avoid perpetrators tracing their child.

See also Chapter 13 *Safety and Confidentiality Issues*.

Registering for health care

School staff may help new parents and pupils by prompting them to register with a new GP and dentist.

Finding a school place for children living in refuges and temporary accommodation: local authorities' obligations

> 'Any change of school or FE college can be a difficult time for a family, but the particular circumstances associated with escape from domestic violence can make it an even more difficult occasion, particularly if there is an appreciable delay before a school or FE college place can be found.'
>
> Department for Education and Skills 2006: 74

When a child moves home, he or she should normally continue at the same school unless it is too far away for travel or unless this would put the child at risk from the abuser. Travel assistance should be given under the local authority's normal arrangements.

If the child needs to attend a new school, the local authority has a duty to find a suitable place, whether the child has moved permanently or temporarily. Local authority fair access protocols typically provide for a place to be found in a fortnight. If all schools are full, the child must be placed above a normal school intake. Children who have special educational needs should be placed quickly and appropriate provision made. Children with challenging behaviour must not be refused admission on the grounds that the child is first to be assessed for special educational needs (Department for Children, Schools and Families (School Admissions Code) 2008b: para 3.31).

> 'All schools and academies must participate in their local authority area's protocol in order to ensure that unplaced children, who live in the home local authority, especially the most vulnerable, are offered a place at a suitable school in the home local authority as quickly as possible. This includes admitting children above the published admission number to schools that are already full.'
>
> Department for Children, Schools and Families (School Admissions Code) 2008b: para 3.44

Refuge workers gave accounts of children who were, nevertheless, out of education for prolonged periods. In these cases, they would have liked previous schools to continue providing work, by email and the internet if necessary. Some refuges have staff who can help children continue their studies until they start a new school.

Chapter 13

Safety and confidentiality issues in schools

Pupil and parent/carer safety and well-being

Every school has responsibility for the safety and well-being of their pupils. This is a priority for vulnerable children, including those experiencing domestic violence. Domestic violence is a child protection issue and all school staff should be aware of current child protection procedures and who is the lead person for this in their school. The school's child protection policy should include reference to domestic violence.

Staff safety procedures

School staff can sometimes be put in very challenging situations, for example, where a father is behaving in a threatening way, having come into school insisting on seeing his child. Every school should have a clear policy on what to do in such circumstances, and all staff should be aware of how to respond.

Schools should follow the guidance set out in the Department for Education and Skills' *Legal Toolkit for Schools* (2002), which gives advice on policy and procedures for responding to violent or threatening behaviour aimed at staff, plus advice about risk assessments. It is available for download from http://publications.teachernet.gov.uk (enter the title in the Search box to locate it).

A poster setting out the potential consequences to visitors who use threatening or abusive behaviour can also be downloaded from the same site.

Perpetrators or alleged perpetrators wanting contact with their children through school

'I had one case where the father was circling the school. A child was frightened to death and didn't want to go in the playground. The father and his new partner had settled nearby.'

A children's counsellor

Perpetrators of domestic violence can be persistent in trying to trace families and make contact against the wishes of the mother. One way they can do this is through schools; an abusive ex-partner who is the parent of a child may give apparently plausible reasons for needing information or seeing the child. Giving out information can put the mother and her child at risk of further harm.

In making decisions that will protect the family from the perpetrator, schools should be aware of the difference between being a 'parent', and having 'parental responsibility'. The following comes from *Domestic Violence and Children: Good Practice Guidelines*.

'Definitions of "parent" in education law

Section 576(1) of the Education Act 1996 defines a "parent" to include:

(a) Anyone with parental responsibility

(b) Anyone who has care of a child

By implication, the Education Act includes all birth parents within its definition of "parent". However, the wide definitions contained in this Act apply only in specific contexts, and are not relevant to schools' practice in all situations.

Definitions of "parental responsibility" under the Children Act

The concept of "parental responsibility" under the Children Act 1989, which is different from the concept of "parent", provides the starting point for schools in considering what rights, if any, a non-resident parent may have in relation to information about a child's schooling. The categories of people included in the concept of "parent" contained in the Education Act 1996 are much wider than those included in the concept of "parental responsibility".

In situations where a non-resident parent who is a perpetrator of domestic violence is attempting to use the school to try to track down a former partner (usually the child's mother), one of the first issues which the school should consider, is whether the non-resident parent has parental responsibility, and whether there is clear legal advice that should be followed.'

James-Hanman 2005: 15

The government web site *Directgov* (http://www.direct.gov.uk) gives information about parental responsibility; unlike mothers, not all fathers have responsibility for their children, under law. The site states:

'A father ... has this responsibility only if he is married to the mother when the child is born or has acquired legal responsibility for his child through one of these three routes:

• (from 1 December 2003) by jointly registering the birth of the child with the mother
• by a parental responsibility agreement with the mother
• by a parental responsibility order, made by a court.

Living with the mother, even for a long time, does not give a father parental responsibility and if the parents are not married, parental responsibility does not always pass to the natural father if the mother dies.'

http://www.direct.gov.uk/en/Parents/ParentsRights/DG_4002954

Where there are concerns about risk to children, schools can check for up-to-date information on the following web sites:

http://www.standards.dfes.gov.uk/parentalinvolvement/pwp/parental_resp/
http://www.teachernet.gov.uk/management/atoz/p/parentalresponsibility/

What schools should do in cases of domestic violence

Any person who has parental responsibility normally has the right to be involved in their child's education. However, there may be circumstances when that right might put a child and the resident parent at risk of harm from a perpetrator of domestic violence. When a school is not clear about the safety of a child they should contact their local authority for legal advice.

Below are example scenarios schools may face that could potentially lead to harm to a child or a mother.

- The mother may have made the school aware that she is worried that her ex-partner, the father of her children, is trying to trace them – or school staff may suspect that this is the case, even if she hasn't disclosed this information.
- Someone may call at the school in person or by phone asking for information about a child, possibly including contact details – they may sound plausible in their enquiry.
- A father may call into school to pick up his child either at the end of the school day or during the day; he is not the person who usually picks the child up, and the receptionist is not sure whether he still lives with the family. The father asserts that he has parental responsibility.
- Photographs of children may be displayed and a visitor, who has an apparently legitimate reason to be in school, is scrutinising them. This is a way former partners have used to trace their children.

For further advice, schools can check on the above web sites or contact their Local Safeguarding Children Board.

Giving out information may result in contact being renewed between a perpetrator and a family escaping domestic violence and may put them at risk.

Information-sharing with the non-resident parent

If an ex-partner with parental responsibility asks for copies of school reports, these can be provided, but without the contact information that might enable him to trace the mother and children. Staff do not have to contact an ex-partner who is unaware that his child attends their school. Sharing information could put the child or the abused parent at risk and might create a situation whereby the perpetrator breaks the terms of a court order (James-Hanman 2005).

Safe information-sharing

Responsible information sharing is essential in enabling organisations and professionals to work together to protect domestic violence victims and their children from harm.

Yet information sharing between professionals can present staff with dilemmas and cause anxiety. On the one hand, inappropriate information sharing can put parents and their children at serious risk, as information that gets into wrong hands could lead to the perpetrator tracking them down. On the other hand, 'it is important to remember there can be significant consequences [in terms of child protection] to not sharing information' (Department for Children, Schools and Families 2008a: 2). This guide contains seven golden rules for information sharing and is available from http://www.everychildmatters. gov.uk/informationsharing

Children going missing from education

Children in families fleeing domestic violence and those who may be pressured into forced marriage are a significant group amongst pupils who go missing from education. For further guidance, see *Identifying and Maintaining Contact with Children Missing or at Risk of Going Missing from Education: Process Steps: Good Practice Guide* (Department for Education and Skills 2004).

Safety issues arising when pupils transfer between authorities or change schools

Families fleeing violence may not wish to provide a former school with information about their new location out of fear of this getting into the wrong hands and leading to them being tracked down. This can present problems with regard to the passing on of records to the new school. Another risk can be when information is passed between professionals who are unaware of potential risks.

To resolve these problems, pupil-tracking teams can be used as an intermediary. School records can be passed on to such teams, then forwarded to the new school. See Chapter 12 for information about the transfer of school records and ContactPoint. There is a secure web site for Common Transfer File from School to School; see http://www.teachernet. gov.uk/s2s

What to do if a member of staff has concerns about the welfare of a child

If a member of school staff has concerns about the welfare of a child, including the impact of domestic violence, whether suspected or known about, then the procedures summarised in the flow chart for referral in *Working Together to Safeguard Children* (HM Government 2006: 142) should be followed. For information about the broad responsibilities proposed for the designated senior person for child protection, consult teachernet: http://www. teachernet.gov.uk/management/atoz/C/childprotection/

Chapter 14

Looking to the future

Educating young people and the community

'Research commissioned by the Home Office ... indicated that for domestic violence to be addressed effectively in schools, it should at the least be a core feature in personal, social and health education (PSHE) and preferably be included across the curriculum.'

House of Commons 2008: 36

'Educational work in school and youth settings needs to start early – at least from the age of eleven and preferably in primary school – if it is to influence the attitudes of a rising generation of young people.'

Mullender *et al.* 2002: 219

Schools are in a unique position to reach into a community and educate people about domestic violence, relationships, forced marriage and 'honour'-based violence. They have a legal duty to promote pupils' moral, spiritual and social development. Education about healthy and safe relationships plays a key part.

In this chapter we will explore:

- how schools can raise awareness of these issues amongst staff, parents and pupils
- why schools should teach about domestic violence, forced marriage, 'honour'-based violence and healthy relationships
- issues related to staff training, and available resources
- what schools can teach about these subjects and to whom
- some teaching guidelines.

Raising awareness: providing information to the community

'Displays of helpful information about such things as national children's helplines (Childline, NSPCC) and peer support schemes for children and young people in easily accessible places (e.g. on pupils' year planners) can encourage them to share concerns.'

Department for Education and Skills 2006: 72

The following are ways to demonstrate to the community that education settings are aware of the harm domestic violence does to children and to help ensure people know where to go for support:

- display posters advertising helplines and make leaflets available. Posters and leaflets, in a variety of languages and aimed at both children and parents, are available from http://www.womensaid.org.uk (some highlight the negative impact on children; important information for parents). The Home Office has produced download-able leaflets and posters, which are available from http://www.crimereduction. homeoffice.gov.uk or can be ordered from the Home Office Publications Order Line 0870 241 4680;
- leave cards with details of local and national helplines and key safety information around school;
- display details of The Hideout, a web site for children and young people created by Women's Aid: http://www.thehideout.org.uk;
- display details of the Refuge web site: http://www.refuge.org.uk;
- place stickers with useful information on the insides of toilet doors;
- make *The Survivor's Handbook* available to the community. This is a comprehensive guide, written for anyone experiencing domestic violence and containing information about its impact on children. It is downloadable from http://www.womensaid.org. uk and available in different languages;
- address the issue in assemblies and on themed days, to which parents, governors and members of the community are invited;
- ensure all staff have received training on domestic violence;
- use the set of materials from Every Child Matters on forced marriage, including leaflets, posters and a card, to raise awareness of the important child protection issues surrounding forced marriage and to provide information about sources of sup-port. The materials can be downloaded from http://www.everychildmatters.gov.uk/ socialcare/safeguarding/forcedmarriage/

Why teach about domestic violence?

On the face of it, domestic abuse may seem like a difficult issue to discuss and teach to young people, yet a wealth of quality resources are available. Schemes of work on the subject have been written for all age groups; it is a recurring theme in soap operas, drama, song lyrics, biographies and autobiographies, including those of celebrities.

Education about domestic violence, including forced marriage and 'honour'-based violence is crucial for the following reasons.

Supporting young people who live with domestic violence and informing them about sources of support

It can be helpful for them to know how common it is, that other young people may suffer similar anxieties to theirs and about organisations and web sites that support others in their situation.

Enabling young people to help each other

Many young people would rather talk to a friend or sibling than to an adult about an abusive home situation, especially as they get older. Almost a third know someone who is experiencing domestic violence, either between their parents or in teenage dating relationships (Mullender *et al.* 2002: 220). They need to know how to support each other.

> 'This is heavy stuff for a child to have in their life and it is arguably unfair to leave young people carrying this burden without some attempt in school to give them a greater understanding of what domestic violence is and to equip them to know what can be done about it.'
>
> Mullender *et al.* 2002: 220

Helping young people to break the silence that surrounds domestic violence

If the subject is rarely discussed or publicised, the underlying message to children is that it is unmentionable. This makes it harder for them to disclose information and seek help.

> 'The teachers aren't recognising it, because it's something they don't talk about. Both teachers and students need to be more aware.'
>
> A family support worker

Informing young people about healthy and safe relationships and preparing them for relationships

There are widespread views amongst young people that violence between partners is acceptable in some circumstances. Mullender *et al.* (2002: 70) found that:

- as many as a third of teenage boys and a fifth of teenage girls agreed with the statement 'some women deserve to be hit';
- over 60 per cent of 13- to 16-year-old boys agreed with the statement 'women get hit if they have done something to make men angry'. A majority of girls agreed with it.

Researchers found that attitudes harden as boys reach their teenage years and highlighted the need for education about perpetrators' responsibility for their own violence and information about dangers such as post-separation violence.

Children need education about equality and non-violent relationships. Some who have grown up with violence may think hitting within families is normal. Some will have observed how violence and fear are effective ways of controlling people.

> 'They should teach about domestic violence. Children grow up thinking violence is right. At the age of ten, my son thought it was right to hit women. He was violent to me.'
>
> A mother

'I've grown up with violence. Violence is all I've ever known.'

A secondary school boy

Abuse in teenage relationships is widespread (see Chapter 3). Young people need to be aware of the signs and recognise when a relationship is becoming abusive. They also need to know what help is available.

'The existence of abuse in teenage relationships further underlines the urgent need for effective early education on domestic violence and relationships.'

House of Commons 2008: 33

Helping young people understand when behaviour towards them is unacceptable and how they can keep themselves safe

The government recommends that pupils should be taught to:

- recognise and manage risks in different situations and decide how to behave responsibly
- judge what kind of physical contact is acceptable and unacceptable
- recognise when pressure from others (including people they know) threatens their personal safety and well-being and develop effective ways of resisting pressure.

HM Government 2006: 68

This guidance states that 'discussions about personal safety and keeping safe can reinforce the message that any kind of violence is unacceptable'. Children and young people should know that it is acceptable to talk about their problems and to be signposted to sources of help.

Supporting young people at risk of being forced into marriage or of 'honour'-based violence

Recent research has found that a great many victims of forced marriage and 'honour'-based violence did not even see themselves as victims, but rather as perpetrators of wrongdoing against their families. Many said that they did not know that their marriage was forced and had no idea where to turn for support or information (House of Commons 2008: 130). Schools can provide a lifeline to vulnerable pupils by providing information on support services.

Reducing bullying

The skills and knowledge gained in work to prevent domestic abuse can influence pupils' behaviour within and outside of school. It can be an effective way of reducing incidents of bullying, for example. Domestic violence can be addressed as part of education about bullying.

Providing much-desired education

Many mothers have said they would like schools to address the issue of domestic violence as it can be a complex one for parents who are victims of abuse to address. The vast majority of secondary age children and a majority of primary age children said they would like lessons on domestic violence in school (Mullender *et al.* 2002: 220). They wanted to:

- understand what it is and why it happens
- know what to do if it should occur
- know how to stop it.

Helping prevent domestic violence

Things that help prevent abusers abusing include:

- understanding the effects of abuse
- peer pressure not to abuse one's partner
- a consistent message from friends, family and all relevant agencies and professionals that domestic abuse is unacceptable and that most of it is criminal
- skills in cooperation and working as equals
- a strong criminal justice response and effective enforcement of any criminal or civil orders against abusers.

Debbonaire et al. 2006

Staff training and teaching resources

A conclusion of the House of Commons Home Affairs Committee was that educating children about domestic violence, 'honour'-based violence and forced marriage should become statutory (House of Commons 2008: 61). The report states:

> 'It is vital that teachers and other education professionals are equipped to teach about domestic violence and forced marriage, recognise signs of abuse and know how to help students.'

The same report states that education professionals cannot be expected to deal confidently and effectively with these subjects without training, guidance and supervision. Teachers have said they would rather not deliver lessons about domestic abuse than deliver them badly.

Resources surrounding the 'Every Child Matters' outcomes

A starting point might be for staff to reflect on the impact of domestic violence in relation to the five Every Child Matters outcomes (see Chapter 6 *Summary – domestic violence and the 'Every Child Matters' Five Key Outcomes*). Excellent resources for staff training and schemes of work for teaching about domestic violence are available to schools. Some provide lesson plans for young people from Reception through the Key Stages. Highly recommended are the following:

Spiralling Toolkit for Safer, Healthier Relationships (Debbonaire *et al.* 2006)
This is a comprehensive teaching toolkit aimed at children and young people aged five and up. It contains information, activities, resources and programmes of work for teachers, designed to help prevent domestic violence and promote gender equality. The accompanying film, Spiralling, is suitable for young people aged 11 and over. It features abuse and control in a relationship between two teenagers. (Both available free and online from Safer Bristol at http://www.bristol.gov.uk/ccm/content/Community-Living/Crime-Prevention/safer-bristol-partnership).

Expect Respect Education Toolkit (2008)
This toolkit is a comprehensive resource, developed by Women's Aid working with teachers, consisting of a 'core' lesson for each year group from reception to year 13, based on themes that have been found to be effective in tackling domestic abuse. There are supporting resources and there is additional online support. (Available free and online from http://www.thehideout.org.uk/over10/adults/resources/educationaltoolkit/default.aspa).

Domestic Violence Prevention Pack for Schools – Promoting Healthy Relationships and Creating Safer Communities.[1] This is a pack with video in four sections as follows:

- Section 1 Introduction to the pack and to domestic violence
- Section 2 What can schools do about domestic violence?
- Section 3 The activities and how to use them
- Section 4 Resources and reference manual

(Available from http://www.westminsterdomesticviolenceforum.org.uk)

Other recommended books/materials include the following.
Safe Learning: How to Support the Educational Needs of Children and Young People Affected by Domestic Violence (Mill and Church 2006)
Published by Save the Children in conjunction with Women's Aid, this booklet is aimed at education and other professionals working with young people affected by domestic violence. It provides practical guidance on how they can be supported and on schools' responsibilities.

Safe and Sound: A Resource Manual for Working with Children who have Experienced Domestic Violence (Saunders and Humphreys 2002)
Published by Women's Aid, this manual is written for refuge children's support workers, but could be a useful resource for staff in education settings supporting children who have experienced domestic violence.

Womankind Worldwide
This campaigning organisation runs a programme for secondary school students and their teachers aimed at raising awareness of, and stopping, violence against women. They provide curriculum materials on violence against women, including a free CD-Rom with 12 personal, social and health education (PSHE), and citizenship lessons for years 9 and 10 looking at healthy relationships and at challenging gender-based violence. http://www.womankind.org.uk/uk-schools.html

Other local authority resources

Many local authorities have developed resources and education packs containing work programmes, activities and DVDs. Most are available online; some are free. The National Union of Teachers (NUT) has published a list: http://www.teachers.org.uk/resources/word/Local_Authority_Resources.doc

The NUT also publishes a booklet, *Silence is Not Always Golden*, containing guidelines on domestic violence for teachers.

When training is being planned, consider the following:

- the subject will raise difficult personal issues for some staff. This should be acknowledged and support made available for those who wish to seek it;
- teaching and raising the profile of the subject is likely to lead to disclosures from young people or parents – staff should feel that they have access to support to help them deal with issues raised;
- non-teaching staff should be included in training. This is important as vulnerable children are often befriended by and may disclose to, accessible adults such as lunchtime organisers, after-school club workers, teaching assistants and librarians. Those staff may be the first to pick up that something is wrong;
- after initial training, staff should have continued access to consultation with professionals, e.g. from domestic violence agencies, educational psychologists and Child and Adolescent Mental Health Services (CAMHS);
- after staff training, their readiness to talk about domestic violence with young people should be evaluated. Some may still feel ill equipped to cope with pupils' responses or questions that may emerge. This will need to be addressed and staff will need support and supervision.

Organisations and professionals that may be able to contribute to staff training include:

- PSHE staff and advisory teachers
- the Local Safeguarding Children Board (LSCB)
- Women's Aid/women's refuges
- representatives from the local Domestic Violence Forum
- voluntary sector services such as Childline, the Children's Society, the NSPCC and Barnardos
- educational psychologists
- CAMHS
- social care professionals.

Teaching about forced marriage and 'honour'-based violence

On the subject of 'honour'-based violence and forced marriage, N. Afzal, Director of Crown Prosecution Service, London West said:

> 'The main obstacle is the lack of awareness, the lack of education, around this issue ... there are still people who are surprised by it. There is a need to make sure that

everybody is familiar with the issues, everybody is aware that this is an issue not of honour, it is an issue of power and control.'

House of Commons 2008: 27

The House of Commons report recommends that 'the DCSF take steps to ensure that all schools are promoting materials on forced marriage, whilst allowing them to retain discretion on the details' (para. 94). There have been suggestions that some schools are wary of 'treading on the toes' of particular communities, so avoid broaching these topics. The report (at para. 95) states:

'We strongly urge the Department to recommend that education on these issues is explicitly made a part of the statutory sex and relationships curriculum, rather than being left to the discretion of individual schools.'

Resources and information on forced marriage are available at: http://www.everychild matters.gov.uk/socialcare/safeguarding/forcedmarriage/

In addition, there is an educational video on marriage and freedom of choice produced by the Foreign and Commonwealth Office for use in schools called *Tying the Knot*. It examines the question of marriage across various cultures and an aim is to promote discussion. To order, contact the FCO's Community Liaison Unit on 020 7008 0135 / 0230 / 0199 or go to www.fco.gov.uk.

Teaching young people about domestic violence

Hester and Westmarland's Home Office Research Study (2005: 11) recommends:

'a cross-curricular approach that includes student-centred interactive lessons on relationships and abuse, visual input such as drama, plus training for teachers and multi-agency support.'

The subject of domestic abuse can and should be covered comprehensively in the PSHE curriculum. As well as being a topic in its own right, it should feature in work on bullying, conflict resolution, children's rights, human rights and gender discrimination.

When teaching, links can be made to the following:

* different topics covered in the Social and Emotional Aspects of Learning (SEAL) materials, for example, *Getting On and Falling Out*; *Say No to Bullying*; *Relationships* (see http://nationalstrategies.standards.dcsf.gov.uk/primary/publications/banda/seal/)
* work on children's rights and responsibilities. See UNICEF's *Little Book of Children's Rights and Responsibilities*: www.unicef.org.uk/tz/resources/resource_item.asp?id=23
* work on disclosing difficult issues
* schools' peer counselling schemes.

Education about domestic abuse should also go beyond the confines of the PSHE/ Citizenship class.

What type of teaching do young people want?

Young people like:

- lessons on relationships and abuse, undertaken in interactive ways
- lessons with visual input such as drama and DVD
- discussion-based classes
- opportunities to ask questions
- lessons that address emotional aspects of relationships including uncomfortable situations such as relationship endings.

What age group should be taught?

Researchers stress that work needs to start at a young age for it to have the most impact; at least from the age of 11 and preferably in primary school. Evaluations of primary school projects indicate this is an effective time to influence children's attitudes.

Some aims of a domestic violence curriculum for children and young people

- To raise awareness about domestic violence and its impact.
- To provide opportunities to learn about healthy relationships and develop skills and confidence to form relationships based on respect.
- To enable young people to see domestic violence as an issue connected with bullying, power and control in relationships.
- To develop knowledge about violence in intimate relationships.
- To develop conflict resolution skills.
- To challenge sexist and/or disrespectful attitudes and behaviour towards the opposite sex.
- To inform young people about sources of help and about their rights to legal and other protection.

Teaching ideas

An assembly or performance can be a good way to introduce the domestic violence topic but such one-off events need to be sustained; the topic can then be explored in PSHE and other lessons.

Large group, themed or cross-curricular activities

- Hold assemblies on domestic abuse and themed days or weeks to mark International Women's Day and National White Ribbon Day to show support for action against domestic violence. Classes or groups can research the topic and make a presentation to the school. The hard-hitting impact of performances and assemblies can spur young people into action. One group decided to further develop their peer mentoring in school as a result of attending a young people's domestic violence conference.
- Show videos that portray how it is for children living with domestic violence and what young people can do about it.

- Invite professionals into schools to talk about their roles and answer children's questions. They could be from:
  — the police domestic violence unit
  — a women's refuge
  — Childline
  — other voluntary sector agencies, e.g. Children's Society, Women's Aid
  — social care
  — the Crown Prosecution Service.
- Invite specialist theatre groups into school that perform plays for young people about domestic violence and will do follow-up workshops.
- Hold a follow-up poster or poetry competition and a poster campaign.

A word of warning: young people who are living with or have lived with domestic violence can find such events distressing. For some, it may be the first time the subject has ever been raised outside the home. This should be acknowledged at the start of any session and pupils informed about who they can approach if affected by the issues. Schools should consider informing parents or carers that the subject is being covered in school.

Cross-curricular teaching and guidelines

Domestic violence is a mainstream issue and, as such, can be addressed in different areas of the curriculum, such as the following.

- *English*: domestic violence occurs in a wealth of children's and adult's literature, both fiction and non-fiction. Many autobiographies describe domestic violence (see below).

Pupils can research gender issues in literature. They can also be asked to read and interpret lyrics from pop songs (see below).

- *Humanities*: historical and cultural beliefs about the rights husbands have had over their wives, and gender attitudes, can be studied; as can Erin Pizzey and the history of the women's refuge movement or the history of organisations such as the NSPCC and Barnardos. See http://www.womensaid.org.uk/
- *Media studies*: various soap operas have covered the theme of domestic violence and power and control in relationships.
- *Music*: many song lyrics make reference to domestic violence.
- *Design, art and craft*: pupils can study what would make a home or refuge safe.

Resources recommended by domestic violence professionals

Following is a selection of books and other resources recommended by domestic violence professionals who work with children, with some examples of how they can be used.

Video and DVD

Home Truths (1999)

A highly recommended 12 minute DVD from Leeds Animation Workshop for children aged eight and above. There is an accompanying booklet containing background information, teaching strategies and ideas for follow-up work (see http://www.leedsanimation.org.uk).

Five separate animated film clips show young people responding positively to different domestic violence situations. Physical, emotional, financial and pet abuse is portrayed as well as the dilemmas young people face. Each young person takes some action: telling friends or a trusted adult; contacting an agency; asserting their right to live in a violence-free environment; telling a teacher. The clips also address some of the myths about domestic violence.

Where is the Love? (2006)

This is a DVD resource pack from Young Voice in partnership with Surrey Youth Development Service (running time 22 minutes). The pack was produced in consultation with young people and is aimed at helping them to address violence and controlling or manipulative behaviour in relationships. The resource comes with guidance on running a session, links to curriculum activities and discussion prompts. The material addresses both male–female and female–male violence.

Watch Over Me II – Relationships and Choices

This pack comprises a teenage soap opera and personal safety programme, originally distributed to all secondary schools and aimed at educating young people about personal safety including domestic violence and forced marriage. There are seven lessons, each 45 minutes long, and each relating to an episode (15 minutes) of the soap. A stated aim is to help teenagers think about paths they choose and decisions they make. The actors are members of the National Youth Theatre of Great Britain. The pack includes background information, lesson plans and worksheets.

Books for young children

Not Now Bernard (D. McKee (1980), Red Fox)

A humorously illustrated story, loved by children of all ages, about a boy whose parents are too busy to understand that he is in danger from a monster that wants to eat him. It provides a wealth of teaching opportunities:

* to explore and experiment with 'feelings' words related to safety, anxiety and neglect;
* to talk about how Bernard might feel about his home circumstances (this can be extended to the situation where domestic violence was happening in the home);
* to reflect on what Bernard could do and who he could he speak to (e.g. someone in school, church, mosque etc);
* to reinforce the idea that children are not to blame;
* to raise children's awareness about other avenues of support, e.g. Childline, The Hideout web site, local support services. A follow-on activity could be to design a poster that Bernard would see in school that could help him.

Where the Wild Things Are (M. Sendak (1963), Harper & Row)

This is a children's classic. Max has adventures when he is sent to bed with no supper and sails away to a land of monsters. The illustrations contain a wonderful range of facial expressions that could stimulate discussion about different feelings and their underlying causes.

Misery Moo (J. Willis and T. Ross (2003), Henry Holt)

A book about trust and relationships; how friendship can weather anything. Somebody feels miserable and someone else keeps trying to cheer them up. This is relevant to how a child living with domestic violence might feel. Children will enjoy the humour.

No Matter What (D. Gliori (1999), Bloomsbury)

A book for young children about the unconditional love between a parent and a child, no matter how hard things get or how you are. 'It's like that with love – we may be close, we may be far, but our love still surrounds us … wherever we are.'

> 'This book … I read it to a child at the end of every session with her. I must have read it about 20 times. She was in and out of care.'
>
> A children's counsellor

Hands are Not for Hitting *(M. Agassi (2002), Free Spirit)* and Words are Not for Hurting *(E. Verdick (2004), Free Spirit)*

These books describe positive and negative uses of our hands, feet and language.

Is it Right to Fight? A First Look at Conflict *(P. Thomas (2003), Hodder Wayland)*

This is a picture book for young children about fights and arguments and how to resolve them. It contains suggestions for discussion and activities to do with individual or a class.

The Feelings Books *(M. Sutherland, Speechmark)*

These books are a series of guidebooks, with an accompanying story, that address distressing feelings or mental states. Each provides underlying psychological theories and ideas for positive responses and activities to help children work through, and communicate, feelings. The books are highly regarded by children's counsellors and can be used in a class or with individual children, by teachers, learning mentors and staff involved in pastoral care. Children can identify with the way characters in the books feel.

Titles in the series include:

- *Helping Children Locked in Rage or Hate/How Hattie Hated Kindness* (2003)

  'My favourite. It's for those children who become frozen and cut off; who've had to lock up their feelings; who think everything is a threat or there is some reason why somebody might be being nice to them and can't be genuine.'

  A children's counsellor

- *Anxious or Obsessive Children/Willy and the Wobbly House* (2001)

  'This is good for children who live with domestic violence. I get them to think about their own wobbly house.'

  A children's counsellor

- *Helping Children with Low Self-Esteem/Ruby and the Rubbish Bin* (2003)
- *Helping Children with Fear/Teenie Weenie in a Too Big World* (2003)
- *Helping Children who Bottle Up their Feelings/A Nifflenoo Called Nevermind* (2001)
- *Helping Children who have Hardened their Hearts or become Bullies/A Wibble Called Bipley (and a few Honks)* (2001)

  'I can't praise these books enough ... there's the common theme of somebody coming along and helping.'

  A children's counsellor

Your Emotions (series) *(B. Moses and M. Gordon (1993), Hodder Wayland)*

This is a series of picture books for young children that look at emotions in an amusing and reassuring way. They contain notes for parents and teachers. Titles include: *I Feel Frightened; I Feel Angry; I Feel Jealous*; and *I Feel Sad*.

Fiction books for young people about domestic violence

Jake's Tower *(E. Laird (2001), Macmillan)*

This is a novel about a boy who lives in fear of his mother's violent boyfriend. It is a gripping and moving story and gives interesting insight into some of the complex issues surrounding the impact of domestic violence and school involvement.

Lola Rose *(J. Wilson (2003), Doubleday)*

Jayni and Kenny's home life is affected by their parents' volatile relationship. When their mum wins the lottery, her response – to escape the situation and set up a new home – puts her and the children at great risk. Their new life seems fraught with problems too. This wonderful book for older readers explores relationship issues, hopes and fears through the eyes of Lola Rose.

Books written for individual work with children

Talking about Domestic Abuse: A Photo Activity Workbook to Develop Communication Between Mothers and Young People *(C. Humphreys et al. (2006), Jessica Kingsley)*

A photocopiable activity workbook for use with children aged nine and up whose families have experienced domestic violence, to help and support them in recovery and moving on, with guidance on appropriate use. The activities are designed around four main themes: talking about personal experiences, building self-esteem; naming feelings and facilitating the mother–child communication.

Talking to My Mum: A Picture Workbook for Workers, Mothers and Children Affected by Domestic Abuse *(C. Humphreys et al. (2006), Jessica Kingsley)*

From the same series, this book is aimed at five- to eight-year-olds and features illustrated activities with animal characters. Themes include: exploration of a range of memories and feelings, including changes in the family's living arrangements, talking about their father or happy times with siblings and friends.

Stop Hitting Mum! Children Talk About Domestic Violence
(A. Mullender et al. (2003), Young Voice)

In this book, young people describe the fear and confusion of living with domestic violence. Those living in violent households may be able to identify with these stories; they also provide adults with insight.

Resources on anger

A Volcano in My Tummy: Helping Children to Handle Anger: A
Resource Book for Parents, Caregivers and Teachers *(E. Whitehouse
and W. Pudney (1997), New Society)*

For ages six to thirteen, this book aims to help children deal constructively with anger. It helps young people distinguish between anger the feeling, and violence the behaviour.

Angry Monster Workbook *(H. Shore (1995), Childswork/Childsplay)*

This is a workbook for ages five to twelve about a boy named Arnold, who learns how to calm the angry monsters that make him lose his cool and get into fights. It includes activities such as puzzles and games to help children understand their anger and learn new skills for expressing themselves.

Work the Anger Out … Without Hurting *(J. Hartman and N. Lang,
Educational Activities)*

This is a CD of songs that can be used with primary children to reinforce the idea that anger is a normal emotion but that it is never acceptable to hurt or intimidate anyone else. It can be used to help challenge the notion frequently advanced by perpetrators that anger underlies their behaviour and that victims provoke them and therefore are responsible for the abuse.

A Solution Focused Approach to Anger Management with Children: A
Group Work Manual for Practitioners *(B. Stringer and M. Mall (1999),
Questions Publishing Company)*

This manual is for use with older primary and secondary school aged children. It helps children explore their difficulties, emphasising their ability to do something about it. Sessions cover the assessment of individual needs and group work.

Resources on anxiety

The Huge Bag of Worries *(V. Ironside and F. Rodgers (1996), Hodder
Wayland)*

This is a funny, reassuring story about an anxious child whose worries follow her round. She feels much better when she has shared them with an adult. It can be used to discuss how to disclose a worry safely, how individuals can safely manage worries and what to do if someone does not respond appropriately. Pupils can create 'worry people' and be encouraged to think about their personal support networks. Reading this book can precede the creation of a 'worry bag' with a child (see Chapter 10). Once the worries are out and in the bag, the child may feel less overwhelmed.

Fergus's Scary Night (T. Maddox (2001), Piccadilly Press)

In this story, a little dog sees shadows and hears noises in the night. Children may identify with his feelings and it can be used to prompt discussion about their own anxieties.

Resources on gender equality

Princess Smartypants (B. Cole (2004), Puffin)

A fairy-tale with a difference. Princess Smartypants does not want to get married. She enjoys being a Ms and fights to preserve her independence.

The Gender Respect Workbook (J. R. Falon (2001), Childswork/ Childsplay)

This book contains group activities to teach non-sexist behaviour to children. It could be used in circle time and for assembly planning.

Other resources

Strong Mothers (A. Peake and M. Fletcher (1997), Russell House Publishing)

A resource for mothers and carers of children who have been sexually assaulted.

Self-Esteem Workbook for Teens (A. Bohensky (2003), Growth Publishing)

A workbook that offers adolescents the skills and concepts to enhance self-esteem and assert themselves effectively.

Looking Glass: A Positive Communication Workbook for Young People (L. Regan, S. Jones and C. Pelling (2002), Russell House Publishing)

This book is useful for learning mentors and school counsellors doing individual therapeutic work. It helps children explore feelings and self-perception and think about relationships and how they want to be treated. There is lots of variety but a simple structure.

Draw on your Emotions *(M. Sunderland and N. Armstrong (1997), Speechmark Publishing)*

This is a practical book for ages six to adult that aims to help people express themselves through drawing. Exercises and pictures aim to ease the process of talking about feelings.

Draw on your Relationships *(M. Sunderland and N. Armstrong (2008), Speechmark Publishing)*

Written for ages six to adult, this book is designed for professionals to help people explore, communicate and learn more about themselves in light of their relationships.

Autobiographical accounts of domestic violence

Once in a House on Fire (Andrea Ashworth (1998), Picador) – a young woman's moving and often humorous account of growing up in northern England in the seventies; it is a portrayal of resilience.

Wasted (Mark Johnson (2008), Sphere) – a memoir of a young man's abusive childhood.

Too Much Too Young: My Story of Love, Survival and Celebrity (Kerry Katona (2007), Ebury).

Daddy's Little Earner: A Heartbreaking True Story of a Brave Little Girl's Escape from Violence (Maria Landon (2008), Harper Element) – the story of a girl forced into prostitution by her father.

Sophia's Story (Susan McKay (1998), Gill & McMillan) – the story of a girl living with a brutal father.

No, Daddy, Don't (Irene Pence (2003), Kensington Publishing) – a story about domestic violence behind closed doors that continued via harassment after a divorce and resulted in a father murdering his two children during a contact visit.

Dragonslippers: This is What an Abusive Relationship Looks Like (Rosalind Penfold (2006), HarperCollins Publishers) – 'This is an excellent resource, not only for women who have experienced domestic violence, but also for the people who work with them and to help raise public awareness of the dynamics of abuse' (Nicola Harwin, Chief Executive, Women's Aid).

Shame (Jasvinder Sanghera (2007), Hodder) – a story about forced marriage and honour violence.

Burned Alive (Souad (2005), Bantam) – the testimony of a woman's survival after an attempted honour killing.

I, Tina: My Life Story (Tina Turner and Kurt Loder (1987), Penguin).

The Color Purple (Alice Walker (2004), Phoenix).

Famous people speaking and writing about their experiences of domestic violence

The web sites http://www.burstingthebubble.com and http://www.thehideout.org.uk provide links to the stories of famous people – including actors, musicians, entertainers, celebrity chefs, writers and sportspeople – who grew up with abuse. Some have been inspired to write songs, articles or books about the impact on their lives. These can be a good way for teachers to introduce and discuss the subject, and to look at how people cope in the face of adversity.

Songs about domestic violence

Domestic violence is – and has been for some time – widely featured in pop songs including those by Suzanne Vega, Stevie Wonder and Tracy Chapman. A web site dedicated to songs related to domestic violence and sexual assault (and survival) is: http://creativefolk.com/abusesongs.html

For teachers, studying and interpreting song lyrics is a popular way to introduce the theme and generate discussion. For example one could play *Thank You* by Jamelia and ask 'What is the message of the song?' The answer could be 'My experience has made me stronger and not ruined my life.'

Artists who have written songs about domestic abuse include: Ms Dynamite, Shania Twain, Pink, Aaliyah, and Red Jumpsuit Apparatus. Red Jumpsuit Apparatus is a male band who have written a song about domestic violence, *Face Down*, and created a pro-women, anti-violence video.

> 'Highly recommended for teenagers. They can see the video on YouTube and read the lyrics. There can be discussion about what message [the band] are giving about domestic violence.'
>
> Children's domestic violence worker

Therapeutic games

Therapeutic games offer another way to help children express their views and feelings and develop social skills. Experienced counsellors suggest that adults should always assess the suitability of the game by playing it themselves first. Games can raise difficult issues and put young people on the spot. They should be used with care and only once a rapport with the young person or between members of a group has been established, and not as a rapport-building exercise. Staff using them should have received training about the facts and myths surrounding domestic violence. Some games are non-competitive, so are appropriate for those with fragile self-esteem.

Young Men and Violence Game – for ages 12–18, this game can help young men to explore and reflect on violence-related issues. Available from Incentive Plus.

The Peace Path (L.M. Barden, Western Psychological Services USA) – for ages 6–14, this board game can be used to teach children about domestic violence and how to deal with it safely.

Talk-It-Out (G. Greenhalgh, Western Psychological Services USA) – a game designed to help teenagers to talk. It addresses a range of issues that affect adolescents.

The Ungame (R. Zakich, Western Psychological Services USA) – for ages five to adult, this non-competitive game encourages young people to share thoughts, feelings and ideas through different topics. A focus is on developing listening skills and appropriate responses.

The Socially Speaking Game (A. Schroeder, LDA) – for ages seven and up, this game is fun and aimed at developing basic social skills; it teaches and reinforces important skills using a variety of problem-solving activities.

All About Me (Barnardos) – a board game that supports the understanding of children of all ages who have experienced trauma and loss such as death and divorce.

Web sites about domestic abuse for young people

http://www.thehideout.org.uk (produced by Women's Aid)
This is the national domestic violence web site for children and young people. It informs and helps them identify whether it is happening in their home. Sources of support are listed and advice given to those who want to help a friend. There is a section on safety planning, quizzes, interactive games and a virtual tour of a refuge. There is a resources section for adults. This is a great resource for those supporting individual children as well as for teachers covering the topic in class.

http://www.burstingthebubble.com
An Australian domestic violence web site for young people. It contains definitions, background information, true stories, personal accounts by celebrities, quizzes and sections on safety planning.

Other web sites for young people

http://www.childline.org.uk
The UK's free 24-hour helpline for children who feel in distress or danger. Trained volunteer counsellors comfort and advise young people.

http://www.missdorothy.co.uk
A charity created by a news presenter who suffered abuse as a child. She has created an interactive learning programme for primary and secondary school age children – Watch Over Me. The web site covers many subjects including abuse, sickness and disability.

Other domestic abuse web sites

http://www.womensaid.org.uk
This is a leading domestic violence charity. It runs a 24-hour helpline and provides information, including that about the risks to children and about refuges and other services. It also runs education campaigns, offers training and publishes resources including posters. Information is provided.

http://www.refuge.org.uk
Refuge provides emergency accommodation for women and children fleeing violence. Some refuges provide for women of particular ethnic or cultural backgrounds. There is an outreach service for women in their homes and a 24-hour helpline run in conjunction with Women's Aid.

http://www.mensadviceline.org.uk
A confidential helpline for men who experience violence from their partners or ex-partners.

http://www.bbc.co.uk/relationships/domestic_violence
Information, help and support for anyone affected by domestic violence.

http://www.pawsforkids.org.uk
A charity based in north-west England designed to support women, children and their pets who suffer from domestic violence.

Other web sites

http://www.cafcass.gov.uk
Cafcass looks after the interests of children involved in family proceedings. It works with children and their families, and then advises the courts on what it considers to be in the best interests of individual children.

http://www.rightsofwomen.org.uk
A site offering free legal advice.

http://www.parentlineplus.org.uk
A national charity that works for and with parents.

http://www.shelter.org.uk
A charity that provides help and advice about finding somewhere to live.

http://www.victimsupport.org.uk
A charity that helps people cope with the effects of crime, including victims of domestic and sexual violence. It provides free and confidential support and information, risk assessment, safety planning and support with reporting incidents to the police.

http://www.southallblacksisters.org.uk
A not-for-profit organisation that provides support and advocacy to Asian and African-Caribbean women experiencing abuse (London-based).

Helplines

Freephone 24-hour National Domestic Violence Helpline (0808 2000 247). It is run in partnership between Refuge and Women's Aid. Language Line and Type Talk are available.

MALE (0808 8010 327). The male advice and enquiry line for men experiencing domestic violence.

Respect (0845 122 8609). A telephone helpline for men wanting help to stop abusing their partners.

Parentline Plus (0808 800 2222). A free 24/7 parents helpline, providing parenting advice and parental guidance, on a wide range of parenting issues.

Childline (0800 11 11). A free and confidential, 24-hour helpline for children in distress.

NSPCC Child Protection Helpline (0808 800 5000). Advice and guidance for anyone who is concerned about the welfare of a child.

Honour Network Helpline (0800 5999 247). Information and advice, including legal advice, about forced marriage.

Note

1 Debbonaire, T (2002) *Domestic Violence Prevention Pack for Schools – Promoting Healthy Relationships and Creating Safer Communities*. London: Westminster Domestic Violence Forum.

Bibliography

Becker, F. and French, L. (2004). 'Making the Links: Child Abuse, Animal Cruelty and Domestic Violence' *Child Abuse Review* 13(6): 399–414.

Behr, H. (1997). 'Groupwork with Parents' in K. N. Dwivedi (ed.) (1997), *Enhancing Parenting Skills: A Guide Book for Professionals Working with Parents*. Chichester: John Wiley & Sons.

Bowker, L., Arbitell, M. and McFerron, J. (1998). *Domestic Violence Factsheet: Children*. Bristol: Women's Aid Federation of England.

Brandon, J. and Hafez, S. (2008). *Crimes of the Community: Honour-based Violence in the UK*. Trowbridge, UK: Centre for Social Cohesion.

Cafcass (August 2007). Domestic Violence Toolkit Version 2. Available online at: http://www.cafcass.gov.uk/publications/policies.aspx

Calder, M. C., Harold, G. T. and Howarth, E. L. (2004). *Children Living with Domestic Violence: Towards a Framework for Assessment and Intervention*. Lyme Regis, UK: Russell House.

Council of Europe (2002). *Recommendation of the Committee of Ministers to Member States on the Protection of Women Against Violence adopted on 30 April 2002 and Explanatory Memorandum*. Strasbourg, France: Council of Europe.

Coy, M., Kelly, L., Foord, J. (2007) *Map of Gaps: The Postcode Lottery of Violence Against Women Support Services*. End Violence Against Women and Equality Human Rights Commission.

Davies, D. (1999). *Child Development: A Practitioner's Guide*. New York: The Guilford Press.

Debbonaire, T. and Walton, K., with contributions from Muralitharan, J. and Manley, B. (2006). *Spiralling Toolkit for Safer, Healthier Relationships: Bristol Domestic Abuse Prevention Project: Information, Activities and Resources for Teachers*. Bristol: Safer Bristol. Available online at: http://www.bristol.gov.uk/ccm/content/Community-Living/Crime-Prevention/safer-bristol-partnership

Department for Children, Schools and Families (2008a). *Information Sharing: Pocket Guide*. Nottingham: DCSF Publications. Available online at: http://www.teachernet.gov.uk/_doc/13022/pocket.pdf

Department for Children, Schools and Families (2008b). *School Admissions Code*. Nottingham: DCSF Publications. Available online at: http://www.dcsf.gov.uk/sacode

Department for Children, Schools and Families (2008c). *Statutory Framework for the Early Years Foundation Stage: Setting the Standards for Learning, Development and Care for Children from Birth to Five*. Nottingham: DCSF Publications.

Department for Education and Employment (2001). *Promoting Children's Mental Health within Early Years and School Settings*. Nottingham: DfEE Publications.

Department for Education and Skills (2002). *A Legal Toolkit for Schools*. London: Department for Education and Skills. Available online at: http://publications.teachernet.gov.uk/default.aspx?PageFunction=productdetails&PageMode=publications&ProductId=DfES%200504%202002&

Department for Education and Skills (2004). *Identifying and Maintaining Contact with Children Missing or at Risk of Going Missing from Education: Process Steps: Good Practice Guide*. Department for Education and Skills. Available online at: http://publications.teachernet.gov.uk/default.aspx?PageFunction=productdetails&PageMode=publications&ProductId=LEA%2F0225%2F2004

Department for Education and Skills (2006). *Safeguarding Children and Safer Recruitment in Education*. London: Department for Education and Skills. Available online at: http://publications.teachernet.gov.uk/

Department of Health (2002). *Women's Mental Health: Into the Mainstream: Strategic Development of Mental Health Care for Women*. Available online at: http://www.dh.gov.uk/en/Consultations/Closedconsultations/DH_4075478

Department of Health (2005). *Responding to Domestic Abuse: A Handbook for Health Professionals*. London: Department of Health Publications. Available online at: http://www.londonscb.gov.uk/files/resources/health_network/responding_to_dv__a_handbook_for_health_professionals.pdf

Doyle, C. (2003). 'Child Emotional Abuse: The Role of Educational Professionals' *Educational and Child Psychology* 20(1): 8–21.

Doyle, R. (1996). *The Woman Who Walked Into Doors*. London: Jonathan Cape.

Edleson, J. (1999). 'The Overlap between Child Maltreatment and Woman Battering' *Violence Against Women* 5(2): 134–54.

End Violence Against Women (2006). *UK Poll of 16–20 Year Olds*. London: ICM. Available online at: http://www.amnesty.org.uk/uploads/documents/doc_17400.pdf

Foreign and Commonwealth Office and Department for Education and Skills (2005). *Dealing with Cases of Forced Marriage: Guidance for Professionals*. London: Forced Marriage Unit. Available online at: http://www.fco.gov.uk/resources/en/pdf/FMarriageGuidance-Education

Gerhardt, S. (2004). *Why Love Matters: How Affection Shapes a Baby's Brain*. Hove, UK: Brunner-Routledge, Taylor & Francis Group.

Glaser, D. (2000). 'Child Abuse and Neglect and the Brain – A Review' *Journal of Child Psychology and Psychiatry and Allied Disciplines* 41(1): 97–116.

Hester, M., Pearson, C. and Harwin, N. (2000). *Making an Impact: Children and Domestic Violence: A Reader*. London: Jessica Kingsley.

Hester, M. and Westmarland N. (2005). *Tackling Domestic Violence: Effective Interventions and Approaches*. Home Office Research Study 290. London: Home Office.

HM Government (2004). *Every Child Matters: Change for Children*. Nottingham: Department for Education and Skills. Available online at: http://www.everychildmatters.gov.uk/_files/F9E3F941DC8D4580539EE4C743E9371D.pdf

HM Government (2006). *Working Together to Safeguard Children: A Guide to Inter-Agency Working to Safeguard and Promote the Welfare of Children*. Published with the permission of the Department for Education and Skills. London: The Stationery Office. Available online at: http://www.everychildmatters.gov.uk/_files/AE53C8F9D7AEB1B23E403514A6C1B17D.pdf

HM Government (2008). *The Right to Choose: Multi-Agency Statutory Guidance for Dealing with Forced Marriage*. London: Forced Marriage Unit. Available online at: http://www.fco.gov.uk/resources/en/pdf/3849543/forced-marriage-right-to-choose

Holden, G. W. and Ritchie, K. (1991). 'Linking Extreme Marital Discord, Child Rearing and Child Behaviour Problems: Evidence from Battered Women' *Child Development* 62: 311–27.

Holden, G. W., Stein, J. D., Ritchie, K. L., Harris, S. D. and Jouriles, E. N. (1998) in G. W. Holden, R. Geffner, and E. N. Jouriles (eds) (1998), *Children Exposed to Marital Violence: Theory, Research, and Applied Issues*. Washington: American Psychological Association.

Home Office (2003). *Safety and Justice. The Government's Proposals on Domestic Violence*. Norwich: The Stationery Office. Available online at: http://www.crimereduction.homeoffice.gov.uk/domesticviolence/domesticviolence37.htm

Home Office (2005a). *Domestic Violence: A National Report*. Available online at: http://www.crimereduction.homeoffice.gov.uk/domesticviolence/domesticviolence51.pdf

Home Office (2005b). *Home Office Development and Practice Report No. 35: Tackling Domestic Violence: Providing Advocacy and Support to Survivors from Black and other Minority Ethnic Communities*. Available online at: http://www.homeoffice.gov.uk/rds/pdfs05/dpr35.pdf

House of Commons, Home Affairs Committee (2008). *Domestic Violence, Forced Marriage and "Honour"-Based Violence: Sixth Report of Session 2007–08*. London: The Stationery Office.

Hughes, H. (1988). 'Psychological and Behavioral Correlates of Family Violence in Child Witnesses and Victims' *American Journal of Orthopsychiatry* 58(1): 77–90

Hughes, H. (1992). 'Impact of Spouse Abuse on Children of Battered Women' *Violence Update* 1(August): 9–11.

Humphreys, C. (2006). *Research and Practice Briefings: Children and Families, no. 14: Domestic Violence and Child Abuse.* London: Department for Education and Skills. Available online at: http://www.york.ac.uk/depts/spsw/mrc/documents/QPB14.pdf

Humphreys, C. and Thiara, R. (2002). *Routes to Safety: Protection Issues Facing Abused Women and Children and the Role of Outreach Services.* Bristol: Women's Aid Federation of England.

Jaffe, P., Wolfe, D. A., Telford, A. and Austin, G. (1986). 'The Impact of Police Charges in Incidents of Wife Abuse' *Journal of Family Violence* 1(1): 37–49.

James-Hanman, D. (2005). *Domestic Violence and Children: Good Practice Guidelines.* London: Home Office. Available online at: http://www.crimereduction.homeoffice.gov.uk/dv/dv08e.pdf

Jarvis, K. E., Gordon, E. and Novaco, R. (2005). 'Psychological Distress of Children and Mothers in Domestic Violence Emergency Shelters' *Journal of Family Violence* 20(6): 389–402.

Jernberg, A. M. and Booth, P. B. (1999). *Theraplay: Helping Parents and Children Build Better Relationships Through Attachment-Based Play* (2nd edn). San Francisco: Jossey-Bass.

Karr-Morse, R. and Wiley, M. (1997). *Ghosts from the Nursery: Tracing the Roots of Violence.* New York: Atlantic Monthly Press.

Kilpatrick, K. L., Litt, M. and Williams, L. M. (1997). 'Post-Traumatic Stress Disorder in Child Witnesses to Domestic Violence' *American Journal of Orthopsychiatry* 67(4): 639–44.

LeDoux, J. E. (1996). *The Emotional Brain.* New York: Simon & Schuster.

Lehmann, P. (1997). 'The Development of Posttraumatic Stress Disorder (PTSD) in a Sample of Child Witnesses to Mother Assault' *Journal of Family Violence* 12(3): 241–57.

Levendosky, A. A., Huth-Bocks, A. C., Semel, M. A., and Shapiro, D. L. (2002). 'Trauma Symptoms in Preschool-Age Children Exposed to Domestic Violence' *Journal of Interpersonal Violence* 17(2): 150.

Local Government Association, ADSS, Cafcass and Women's Aid (2006). *Vision for Services for Children and Young People Affected by Domestic Violence: Guidance to Local Commissioners of Children's Services.* London: LGA Publications. Available online at: http://www.lga.gov.uk/lga/aio/1224298

McCloskey, L. A., Figuerado, A. J. and Koss, M. P. (1995). 'The Effects of Systemic Family Violence on Children's Mental Health' *Child Development* 66(5): 1239–61.

McGee, C. (2000). *Childhood Experiences of Domestic Violence.* London: Jessica Kingsley.

McIntosh, J. (2002). 'Thought in the Face of Violence: A Child's Need' *Child Abuse and Neglect* 26(3): 229–41.

Maslow, A. (1970). *Motivation and Personality.* New York: Harper & Row.

Mezey, G. (1997). 'Domestic Violence in Pregnancy' in S. Bewley, J. Friend, G. Mezey (eds) (1997), *Violence Against Women.* London: RCOG Press.

Mill, J. and Church, D. (2006). *Safe Learning: How to Support the Educational Needs of Children and Young People Affected by Domestic Violence.* London: Save the Children, and Bristol: Women's Aid Federation of England.

Morley, R. and Mullender, A. (1994). *Preventing Domestic Violence to Women. Policy Research Group Crime Prevention Unit Series, Paper no. 48.* London: Home Office Police Department.

Mullender, A., Hague, G., Imam, U., Kelly, L., Malos, E. and Regan, L. (2002). *Children's Perspectives on Domestic Violence.* London: Sage.

Murray, L. and Cooper, P. (1997). 'Postpartum Depression and Child Development' *Psychological Medicine* 27(2): 253–60.

Murray, L. and Andrews, E. (2000). *The Social Baby.* London: Richmond Press.

Niven, L. and Ball, M. (2007). *National Evaluation of Sure Start.* Nottingham: DfES Publications.

NSPCC Inform, The Online Child Protection Resource: Izzidien, S. (2008). *"I Can't Tell People what's Happening at Home": Domestic Abuse within South Asian Communities: the Specific Needs of Women, Children and Young People: Executive Summary.* London: NSPCC. Available online at: http://www.nspcc.org.uk/inform/research/findings/icanttellsummary_wdf57875.pdf

Perry, B. (1997). 'Incubated in Terror: Neurodevelopmental Factors in the "Cycle of Violence"' in J. D. Osofsky (1997), *Children in a Violent Society*. New York: Guilford. pp. 124–49.

Pynoos, R. S. and Eth, S. (1986). 'Witness to Violence: The Child Interview' *Journal of the American Academy of Child and Adolescent Psychiatry* 25(3): 306–19.

Quinlivan, J. (2000). 'Study of Adolescent Pregnancy in Western Australia' in Partnerships Against Domestic Violence (ed.) (2000), *The Way Forward: Children, Young People and Domestic Violence: Conference Proceedings*. Office of the Status of Women, Canberra. pp. 53–8.

Rai, D.K. and Thiara, R.K. (1997) *Redefining Spaces: The Needs of Black Women and Children Using Refuge Services in England: Their Feelings, Needs and Priority Areas for Development in Refuges*. Bristol: Women's Aid Federation of England.

Refuge (2005). *Refuge Assessment and Intervention for Pre-School Children Exposed to Domestic Violence, August 2005: Under 5s at Significant Risk from Effects of Domestic Violence*. London: Refuge. Available online at: http://www.refuge.org.uk/cms_content_refuge/attachments/Effects%20of%20domestic%20violence%20on%20pre-school%20children.pdf

Rossman, B. B. R., Mallah, K., Dominguez, M., Kimura, S. and Boyer-Sneed, B. (1994). *Cognitive and Social Information Processing of Children in Violent Families*. Paper presented at the annual meeting of the American Psychological Association, Los Angeles.

Saunders, A. (1995). *It Hurts Me Too: Children's Experiences of Domestic Violence and Refuge Life*. London: Childline/Women's Aid Federation of England.

Saunders, H. and Humphreys, C. (2002). *Safe and Sound: A Resource Manual for Working with Children who have Experienced Domestic Violence*. Bristol: Women's Aid Federation of England.

Schore, A. (2001). 'The Effects of Early Relational Trauma on Right Brain Development, Affect Regulation, and Infant Mental Health' *Infant Mental Health Journal* 22(1–2): 201–69.

Shah-Kazemi, S.N. (2001) *Untying the Knot: Muslim Women, Divorce and the Sharia*. Nuffield Foundation, The Signal Press.

Stallard, P. (2003). *Think Good – Feel Good: A Cognitive Behaviour Therapy Workbook for Children and Young People*. Chichester: John Wiley & Sons.

Stringer, B. and Mall, M. (1999). *A Solution Focused Approach to Anger Management with Children: A Group Work Manual for Practitioners*. Birmingham: Questions Publishing Company.

Sutherland, M. (1999). *Helping Children Locked in Rage or Hate: A Guidebook*. Bicester, UK: Speechmark Publishing.

Terr, L. C. (1991). 'Childhood Traumas – An Outline and Overview' *American Journal of Psychiatry* 148(1): 10–20.

Thiara, R. (2005) *The Need for Specialist Domestic Violence Services for Asian Women and Children*. London: Imkaan.

Walby, S. and Allen, J. (2004). *Domestic Violence, Sexual Assault and Stalking: Findings from the British Crime Survey*. Home Office Research, Development and Statistics Directorate. London: Home Office. Available online at: http://www.homeoffice.gov.uk/rds/pdfs04/hors276.pdf

Warren Dodd, L. (2004). *The Effects of Domestic Violence on Mothers and their Young Children and the Development and Evaluation of Groupwork with these Families*. Thesis for the degree of Doctorate in Educational Psychology, University of Manchester.

Webster-Stratton, C. and Hammond, M. (1990). 'Predictors of Treatment Outcome in Parent Training for Families with Conduct Problem Children' *Behaviour Therapy* 21: 319–37.

Weinberg, K. and Tronick, E. (1998). 'Emotional Care of the At-Risk Infant: Emotional Characteristics of Infants Associated with Maternal Depression and Anxiety' *Paediatrics* 102(5): 1298–304.

Weissberg, R. (2000). 'Improving the Lives of Millions of School Children' *American Psychologist* 55(11): 1360–73.

Wolak, J. and Finkelhor, D. (1998). 'Children Exposed to Partner Violence' in J. Jasinski and L. Williams (eds) (1998), *Partner Violence: A Comprehensive Review of 20 Years of Research*. Thousand Oaks, CA: Sage.

Index

Entries for illustrations, tables and text boxes are in *italic*.